Architecture of the World

D0752297

Roland Martin
Henri Stierlin (Ed.)

Greece

Photos: Henri Stierlin
Preface: Max Bill

Benedikt Taschen

Editor of Series   Henri Stierlin
Plans   Jean Duret FAS SIA
English Translation   Kenneth Martin Leake

©   for this edition: Benedikt Taschen Verlag GmbH
©   Compagnie du Livre d'Art, S.A.
Editions Office du Livre, Lausanne
Printed in Germany
ISBN 3-8228-9308-0

Contents

My Connections with Greek Architecture

Preface by Max Bill

At school we learned a good deal about the Greeks – their wars, their philosophy, their poetry, and our study of Greek art brought us into contact with their sculpture, vases and temples.

My first encounter with 'Greek architecture' was the Town Hall of my native city, Winterthur, built by Gottfried Semper. I learned to value this building both as neo-Classic architecture and as an example of a completely balanced interior and exterior: columns, staircases and masonry were all in harmony. It was certainly an imposing structure, but, in fact, far removed from Greek architecture, as I was to discover later on.

In 1935 I came to Paris and saw the Bourse, the Madeleine and the Louvre. Everywhere the formal canon of Greek architecture was applied – to every house and every balcony. In 1926 I arrived in Rome and saw St Peter's, the colonnades, and the Porta Pia. Everything was rooted in the Greek heritage, transposed at several removes to form the inspiration both for palazzi and ordinary doorways. Finally, in 1927, I came to Berlin. The flood of so-called Greek continued there in the Reichstag, the Brandenburg Gate, the Schloss at Charlottenburg, and the long streets with their long façades. Perhaps Henry van de Velde was right when he declared war on columns.

I was no longer so ill-prepared for what was happening. Art history was no longer the only means to teach me that both Renaissance and Empire cabinets and all their imitations may be recognized by their wooden columns. At the same time, a book landed on my table – Le Corbusier's 'Vers une architecture.' In it the author wrote of the Acropolis and the lessons that could be drawn from it. At that time we had become young rationalists. Le Corbusier himself had opened the eyes of many of us, even regarding the essential point of Greek architecture.

3

Project for monument to the unknown political prisoner, by Max Bill, 1951

Hochschule für Gestaltung, Ulm, by Max Bill: corridor linking students' quarters with lecture rooms. 1953-55

Nevertheless, it seems that his remarks and experiences had infinitely more value for himself, as every aesthetic experience is of far greater significance to the person directly concerned.

Although Le Corbusier endowed me with second sight, my own observations were necessarily based on the use of Greek forms made by Renaissance and neo-Classic architects.

In the summer of 1928, when I was still not twenty years old, I first set eyes on Greek buildings. It was the morning of what was to be a hot day and I thought I understood why the Greeks had abandoned the marshy, mosquito-ridden ground where I stood. I was at Paestum, looking at the basilica and the Temple of Neptune, and I remember how much I regretted that these buildings had lost their roofs. What

surprised me most about them was their solidity, not only their geometrical outlines, but their massiveness and the use of materials. I had been used to a progressive lightening of solid buildings from the Renaissance up to the neo-Classic period and the classicism of Auguste Perret's reinforced concrete architecture. Yet here these columns rested directly on the ground and were finished off with a redoubtable flat slab surmounting a slight cushion. Above this slab lay the full weight of the building.

The proportions amazed me still more. Measured frontally, the ratio of the inter-columniation to the diameter of the shafts was 6:5. More incredible still was the ratio to the height of the capital – 3:2. Such large-scale dimensions and the enclosed nature of the masses were completely new and strange experiences for me. It seemed to me a waste of materials, beautiful in itself and imposing, but quite pointless. In 1931 I visited the Temple of Concord at Agrigento and experienced the same feeling as at Paestum: this was a fine building from the technical and constructional point of view, but alien, sunk in false images and all the erroneous developments that have been inherited from Greek prototypes.

I learned with surprise and to my advantage that the breakwaters at Porto Empedocle were made of the drums of columns and wall fragments from the nearby temples, thus endowing them with some practical use. I only experienced slight regret for the disappearance of these monuments – more for their historical significance than for their aesthetic message.

Since then the outlook has changed. The rational architecture of our dreams took an unhoped for flight, quantatively at least, thanks to modernist decoration, the romantic aspect of reinforced concrete, and absence of weight. Total boredom resulted. Rational architecture as such barely succeeded in materializing. Modern architecture became degenerate before it was able to manifest itself in a suitable form.

This possibly explains why the lesson of classical Greek architecture is so much more important than thirty years ago. Having ceased to be directly available it has acquired an important analogous significance. The analogies lie in aesthetic experience, the rigid nature of architectural construction, and the basic cause of the mistake: the false application of a fundamental lesson – order, harmony and reason expressed as a visible unity.

In 1965 I scaled the Acropolis for the first time. The Acropolis rises amid the commotion of modern Athens as a witness of this distant, alien civilization. It has no common bond with our present age and no connection with the people who live in its shadow and practise a religion so different from the one which brought it into being. The ruins stand aside like harbingers on the formidable rock, and it is with a sense of wonder that we survey this city with its countless remains of every architectural tradition from Greek to Renaissance, neo-Classical to popular. It is impossible to avoid thinking that it might have been preferable not to have distributed these architectural forms around the world.

Amid the buildings surmounting the Acropolis, everything appears quite different: there is great spatial and rhythmic unity. They stand apart, but in another sense: the buildings of the present lie as far below. Up above there

Pavilion composed of prefabricated section. Swiss National Exhibition, Lausanne, 1964

continues an important lesson in aesthetics situated outside time and based on order, proportion, and space. To prove this, I can stand between two rows of columns and note how they frame the landscape. From the side they conceal it, for, thanks to their perspective, they present a surface through which the light penetrates by invisible gaps. On the other hand, if I turn sideways, I can see between the rows. I think that this simultaneously closed and open space is one of the most significant experiences that Greek temple architecture can offer us today.

I have seen only temple architecture in Greece; the rest is only known to me in pictures. The temples are significant architectural types and have probably exerted a very powerful influence. Nevertheless, the Greeks also built other kinds of building and lived in simple congenial houses, probably much the same as today. In times of war they built magnificent, large-scale fortresses; indeed, I was unaware how finely built they were before I saw the picture in this book. They also built theaters, including the splendid examples still surviving at Epidaurus, Dodona and Segesta. Their dimensions were dictated by their functions. We may learn from the layouts of both temples and theaters, and finally, I must recall the villages, especially those in the Cyclades, whose unified plans seem singularly up-to-date.

I have had to base this preface on my own personal experiences. It seems to me impossible to evaluate Greek architecture objectively, and the lesson I have drawn from Greece may also be subjective. If this were otherwise, our contemporary architecture might have been very different and might have sustained a better comparison with that of classical Greece.

Granite column in 3 octagonal sections, by Max Bill
Height: 13.9 feet.   Diameter: 2 feet

1. Historical and Intellectual Background

The Greeks found the inspiration and interpretation of their architecture in the political and historical background which it reflected. It was primarily an urban architecture expressive of the city state whose size was restricted both in practice and theory. In their towns, the Greeks devized and applied social, economic and political frameworks most suited to the human development of the citizens.

Influence of society

Greek architecture was first and foremost the expression of a community and, more especially in its early stages, of the basic ties assuring unity. These were, in fact, religious connections from which stemmed the essential development of the temple, the dwelling place of the gods and goddesses who watched over everything. Whether the temple belonged to the god of one city, was a shrine shared by several states or served the whole of Greece, as at Delphi and Olympia, its architectural characteristics remained unchanged and its permanence was assured by the importance of the cult it served. Thus, the first crude examples of Greek architecture in the 9th century B.C. took the form of chapels with simple rectangular or irregularly shaped shrines sometimes divided into two aisles by a central row of pillars. These were first built of wood and later in stone. Great religious buildings of vast dimensions did not come into being before the early 6th century. In the west they were in the heavy Doric style, and in the east favored the rich, complex designs of Ionian architecture, as exemplified in the temple of Artemis at Ephesus and the temple of Hera on Samos.

The basic law of the political group forming the city or 'polis' was the maintenance of independence and autonomy. This meant the autonomous life of the group within its setting and its geographical frontiers, within its city and its surrounding territory along with its social and political structure, economic resources, artistic traditions and the monetary independence which was the prerogative of the most prosperous city states from the late 6th century onwards.

The life and liberty of the group answered those of the individual and exercised their influence over him. Thus architecture was primarily expressive of unity and group life rather than concerned with the problems of individual members of the city. Defensive walls and administrative buildings devoted to politics and commerce – agoras, assembly halls, markets and porticoes – absorbed the city's resources, and the citizen's private houses and their individual comforts were not as yet the subject of architectural experiment. Even in the late 5th century, after the great achievements of the classical period, Alcibiades caused a scandal at Athens by commissioning a painter to decorate the interior walls of his house. The need for autonomy, the expansion of the group's political conscience and the development of institutions whose aim was to ensure the independence of the 'polis' and its community led to the erection of fine city walls from the late 6th century onwards, and influenced the layout and construction of the first architectural centers. These took the form of neighboring buildings grouped round a public square or the shrine of a protecting deity. These squares or 'agoras' soon became the symbols of autonomous Greek city states.

Elements of town planning

Gradually, in the course of the 5th and 4th centuries, theaters and gymnasia became separated from the original center which was also the setting for performances and games closely linked with religious life. Although they gained individual architectural characteristics, they still remained basic elements of the Hellenic town plan. Both in Platonic theory and in accordance with the eyewitness account of Pausanias, there was no Greek city without an acropolis, an agora, a theater, or a market.

The origins and developments of Greek town-planning shared the same background. Presocratic philosophers, meditating on the nature of man and his place in society, ended by resolving theories regarding the best forms of background against which he could discover elements favorable to his development. The first political theorists were also the first town planners who, like Hippodamus of Miletus, outlined town plans which enabled a city's functions to be carried out in the most harmonious setting possible.

A radical change in Greek architecture took place between the 4th and 3rd centuries B.C. This was not so much a formal modification as a basic alteration of inspiration and outlook. The architecture of city states gave way to that of kings and princes. Superficially this may have seemed no more than a question of larger-scale buildings and a development in decoration as opposed to architecture, resulting in a loss of sensitivity. Yet the architecture as a whole and the principles of composition revealed a completely different attitude. The great buildings in the cities were no longer merely group expressions, but also symbolized princely power. They took on a completely new aspect, becoming means of influence, signs of civilization, instruments of diplomacy and conquest. In Alexandria and Pergamon, in the great cities of Asia Minor and the Middle East and in the hellenized towns of Africa, there developed a large-scale prestige architecture to suit the size of the new world opened up to Hellenism by the conquests of Alexander the Great.

Such a background of political prestige directed architects to the production of more individual works. A taste for fine houses came into being. Starting during the 4th century, private building in cities like Alexandria and Pergamon was concentrated on individual houses and particular zones. Space was found for residential quarters, palaces and huge houses for important court officials and rich merchants who assured the economic prosperity of these cities. About the same time new, large-scale forms of funerary architecture came into being. These had been unknown since Mycenaean times and spread through all quarters of the Roman world till the end of the Empire.

A town was no longer merely the center of a small city state. It now played the part of the capital of a vaster world and its proportions increased to a scale commensurate with this new pretension. Its plan and buildings were now on a monumental scale, its squares assumed an architectural unity hitherto unknown and a new aesthetic standard was applied to its streets based on the part played by façades, colonnades and the mingling of perspectives engineered by the use of flanking porticoes and terminated by decorative buildings. This taste for the monumental increased in relation to the ambitions of the city and its ruler. It served as a reflection of their power and the part played by them in a world conquered by Hellenism less by virtue of its political structure than by the strength and quality of its civilization.

Yet in this lay the root of the evil which ended in the dispersal of the original characteristics of Hellenic creativity. By abandoning the balanced restricted setting for which it had been created, and adapting itself to the scale of this new world, Greek architecture lost its most original feature – its fundamental relationship to mankind. It broke up into separate elements which were easy enough for neighboring or later civilizations to copy, but were no longer held together by an ideal unity. It was dissolved and diluted by its extension, and handed over its forms and constructions to another world which changed and integrated them with the new needs and ideals of the Roman Empire.

The formation of city states

With her city states Greece achieved a balanced harmony between the disintegrating nomadic or semi-nomadic countries of central and northern Europe and the centralized bloc of the kingdoms of the East. This harmony favored the development of mankind and the expansion of every variety of art connected with the human species. It may be that this political individuality of the Greeks originated in the geographical structure of the country, with its division into small plains, valleys and innumerable islands. Or, again, these strongly defined zonal differences may have been due to the nature of the establishment of the Greek peoples who arrived in successive waves from the East and were then sustained by migrations, usually towards the West. However this may have been, from early times this individualism was made apparent by the sealing off of priviliged territories including the Attic peninsular, Argos and its gulf, and Sparta with the fertile valley of the Eurotas. In this way, the geographical elements of the states were very soon clearly defined. The city state, considered as a political group, consisted of a town frequently formed as the result of a union of several villages, all or some of whose inhabitants were transferred to the political center of the newly formed state. The town, however, was not separated from its surrounding territory whose boundaries were fixed by the lines of hills which were sometimes very close.

This constricted setting did not prevent violent political or social crises from arising during the states' formation. Throughout the development period of the 7th and 6th centuries, when individual families gave way to coordinated groups, there were frequent and fierce struggles. The states were originally based on the association of a few powerful families who provided the members of the council, one of whom assumed supreme authority, especially in the military sphere. This continuity was based on ownership of land and the council was primarily the meeting place of the great landowners. Some of the Dorian states remained at this stage and maintained a strongly aristocratic character; they were diehard conservatives, opposed to all forms of social evolution, closed to external influences and completely chauvinistic. Sparta and the city states of Crete and Thessaly were the best examples of such oligarchic regimes.

The trend towards colonization was one of the earliest signs of this reaction. From the late 8th century onwards, bands of citizens, unable to find a place in the excessively rigid framework of a state exclusively dominated by family groups firmly attached to their property and prerogatives, set sail overseas. They were responsible for the first conquests of Hellenism by creating colonial cities whose prosperity helped to contribute considerably to the record of Greek architecture and town planning. Among their achievements we may note the temples at Selinunte and Agrigento, Paestum and elsewhere in southern Italy, and the ramparts of Syracuse.

Colonization did not prevent crises from occurring in the city states of the mother country. Fierce and bloody struggles occurred between classes split by need and variations of income. At several points in the Greek world lawgivers arose to codify the primitive laws which were often handed down by word of mouth; heads of clans were the sole trustees of these laws and thought to ensure their stability by invoking their divine origin. Among the most famous and successful of these lawgivers were Solon of Athens, Zaleucus of Locri, and Charondas of Catania. Their codes only proved effective by just and vigorous application and this was ensured by the tyrants. They followed the lawgivers of the clans often to the benefit of the common people by means of a political program which was based on securing their own prestige. The results favored the architectural development of their cities. The names of the Peisistratids at Athens, the Cypselids at Corinth, Cleisthenes of Sicyon, and Polycrates of Samos are all connected with great architectural creations. The tyrants also formulated and realized the earliest town planning programs.

The emergence of democratic regimes

Expansion of commercial resources and the increased range of classes benefiting from this new source of revenue led to a growing opposition to the power of the tyrants; and the final victory of the city states over the Persian forces at Marathon and Salamis opened the way to the development of democratic regimes. The middle classes came to power supported by leaders often descended from the old families crushed or banished by the tyrants. Athens offers a particularly good example of this form of political evolution.

After the fall of the Peisistratids in 510, the fortunes of the democratic party were controlled by Cleisthenes, a member of the Alcmaeonid family which had been banished by the tyrants; he had, however, been shrewd enough to win the favor of the Pythia at Delphi by ensuring the completion of the temple of Apollo about 515. This was the start of the rise of Athens which continued under the inspired guidance of leaders, including Themistocles, Aristeides and Cimon and achieved fruition with the Periclean age.

The workings of the regime were basically

ensured by elections and the drawings of lots. The ten prytaneis or presidents, one for each tribe, who were endowed with executive powers, were chosen by lot. They presided over the council, whose members were also chosen by lot, being responsible for its actions, and also controlling the debates of the popular assembly or ecclesia which was made up of all citizens officially enrolled on the registers of their deme. All laws and important decisions were referred to the vote of the assembly during the normal sessions or in the course of special ones in cases of emergency. Schemes for the future, however, were drawn up and regulated by the council whose political powers were complemented by its judiciary privileges. The popular tribunal, the heliaea, came under the power of the assembly. The nine archons or chief magistrates were also chosen by lot, together with the holders of most other offices. The only posts filled by election were those demanding some technical skill, particularly those concerned with building. If a magistrate was responsible for financial expenditure he had to render an account of his administration before a committee of inspection on his retirement from office. His liabilities were covered by his own property and even by his own life, and he could not leave the state before receiving a ratification of his term of office.

The privileges of the upper classes within these institutions now diminished. Class distinctions had been defined by Solon to accord with listed incomes but were no longer reliable owing to newly developed revenues. Moreover, the new system of tokens of attendance enabled the humblest citizen to hold political or judicial office and to take part in the games and theatrical performances which were part of the great religious festivals. The poor also formed an important class, but their political rights ensured a basic difference between them and the metics, a class of foreigners subject to taxes and special regulations, and the vast body of slaves. The latter were an essential feature of the social and economic organization of the Greek city states and form an important element in any study of labor problems and prices of building construction.

Though the influence of Athens allowed the extension of democratic government to many other city states, the Dorian territories remained deeply attached to the oligarchic and aristocratic tendencies of Crete and Sparta. The citizen assembly and council of elders directed state affairs, but there were important limitations to their powers. As in the Homeric world, only those citizens who carried arms could be members of the assembly and membership of the council or gerousia was, as its name suggests, settled by age limits. Moreover, the real executive power was not vested in the assemblies but in a college of magistrates known as the ephors in Sparta and the cosmi in Crete. Young and old alike were rigidly subjected to the state which imposed strict rules and long periods of military service. These forms of government, apart from the archaic period in Crete and Sparta, did not favor architectural development.

The Hellenistic period

The progressive decline of the Greek city states in the late 4th century, contemporary with and partially related to the growing power of the kingdom of Macedon under Philip and Alexander the Great, brought about a radical transformation of the historical background, which also affected architecture.

We should not unreservedly accept the assertions of Demosthenes regarding the barbarous habits and lack of culture of the Macedonian kings. The excavations now in progress at Pella corroborate the claims of Philip and Alexander to be representatives of Hellenic culture: they help to confirm the evidence of literary texts and reveal a highly developed feeling for art and luxurious aids to everyday life. The fine private houses of Pella with their peristyle courts and huge rooms paved with abstract, geometrical mosaics and enlivened with powerful representations of hunting scenes designed with technical assurance by the best artists, formed a setting for a mode of life endowed with taste and refinement.

They show that Alexander's conquests were more than brilliant military successes; they also ensured the penetration of Hellenic culture as far as the river Indus. Hellenistic art, philosophy and culture made contact with native civilizations, assumed new forms and impressed itself on the cities of the East. The magnificent texts of Asoka and the excavations now in progress in Afghanistan reveal fresh aspects of this vigorous brand of Hellenism. The building of cities and the foundation of Macedonian colonies formed the background to this expansion of Greek traditions, and were the mainsprings of the enrichment of life in which architecture played a great part.

In Greece itself, life in the city states continued apparently unchanged, but, in fact, creative powers were dulled and resources were often greatly reduced. Praiseworthy efforts were made to embellish and enlarge the architectural setting, but the programs were often over-ambitious compared with available means. Traditional architectural forms became impoverished and techniques were not adjusted to suit conceptions based on a grander scale. This period witnessed the rise of the euergetes, or benefactors, who came to the aid of the wavering city states, though not wholly without disinterested motives. They included princes, wealthy merchants and foreign kings who revived the declining workshops with their private funds; and pediments were now inscribed with their names instead of those of the cities in which they stood.

After Alexander's death his rival generals gave full rein to their ambitions, but, after a confused period of struggle, there emerged a regrouping attended by a semblance of balance. Independent and rival kingdoms were established by the Antigonids in Macedonia, the Seleucids in the south, the Ptolemies in Egypt, and the Attalids in Pergamon, and competition between them was not confined to the spheres of politics and war but also extended into the field of the arts. Their towns and capital cities now became the chief art centers and the Greece of city states gave way to one of principalities. Political power was concentrated on the rulers, who were their own army commanders, and administered their domains by representatives or governors who were wholly subservient to them. In those cases where there was still a semblance of an assembly, it possessed no real power. The arts no longer served the community but were dedicated to the ruler and his representatives. Commissions were inspired by the necessities of personal glory and dynastic pressures and were also means of securing political influence, especially in the case of the famous cities of antiquity and the great religious sanctuaries. Large sums of money could be available if the rulers so desired and they were solely responsible. The workshops were no longer, or hardly ever, dependent on the state's resources or the votes of the assembly. This was the background which witnessed the creation and development of Hellenistic monumental architecture.

There were many instances of revival and development throughout the Greek world, especially where rival or neighboring civilizations made contact. In the west, the Hellenic world was too military in character owing to its being forced to repel the attacks of the Carthaginians: it did no more than follow formulae predating the conquerors who were overrunning it. In the east, on the other hand, Hellenism was enriched by the addition of oriental features. A special example of this was the contact between Greek artists and architects and Achaemenid artists who worked for the satraps of Asia Minor, particularly those prolific patrons, King Mausolus and Queen Artemisia of Caria. According to Vitruvius, the palace of King Mausolus at Halicarnassus combined Achaemenid techniques, such as polished brick, with Hellenistic forms of decoration. Temples throughout the country were provided with architectural adornments in the Hellenistic style, the most elaborate example being the famous mausoleum of Halicarnassus. These contacts resulted in a fresh outburst of creativity. The easterners swiftly assimilated Greek culture, adopted the language and institutions of the Greeks, summoned their artists and became their pupils and disciples. Such was the strength of Hellenism in the east that its widespread influence in architectural composition was felt far into the future.

Religious beliefs

Both the starting point and development of Greek architecture were basically linked with religious traditions and beliefs. The gods were closely connected with every aspect of Greek life and thought. According to Hesiod, there were fifty thousand of them on the earth concerning themselves with human problems. Thus their influence must have been powerfully felt within their temples, in the corporate life of the state and in the private lives of its members.

There was a very strict hierarchy within the Greek pantheon. Zeus, 'master of gods and men,' only gained this position after violent struggles with the old established divinities of Chaos. With his wife, Hera, he reigned over Olympus and the Olympian deities who included Apollo, Artemis, Demeter, Aphrodite, Dionysus, and Pluto. They received their functions and attributes in a world where order or cosmos was on a parallel level to that which established the rule of law in the city states. Their powers were often enlarged at the expense of minor divinities whose names they often took over as their own epithets to diversify their attributes and rituals. The great gods formed the basis of an official religion associated with political order and guaranteeing justice. In addition, they exerted a panhellenic influence connected with the great sanctuaries. Zeus at Olympia, Apollo and Dionysus at Delphi, Apollo and Artemis on Delos, and Poseidon in the isthmus of Corinth all attracted games and crowds who surged to the panhellenic festivals in their several seasons. These federal shrines of varying importance were vital elements in the religious and political life of the Greek city states and their architecture reflected their different functions.

A host of minor deities, demigods and heroes sustained popular devotion under the watchful protection of the great gods. In them the common people found a level of belief better adapted to their immediate needs and the everyday life. Changing and different occupations were protected by numerous divinities: Elutheia presided over birth, Hecate and Hermes accompanied the souls of the dead; the Dioscuri watched over sailors, Pan could bring about the rout of an army. Theseus favored Athenian unity, Hercules was the protector of the Dorian migrations. Throughout the Greek countryside, temples, chapels, oratories and altars, differing in design and decoration, formed the natural expression of these popular beliefs.

We have to specify the beliefs relating to death and the life of souls in the hereafter as they involved the creation of original types of funerary monuments. Ever since the early migrations in the Mycenaean periods, domed tombs bore witness to the care taken to ensure that a dead man enjoyed a setting worthy of his life on earth. The moment of death, it was thought, resulted in a harsh separation of the body from the life force, or psyche, which escaped and took refuge in the dark domain of the dead, the kingdom of the shades beyond the Styx. The rites prescribed for the moment of death were essential as they alone secured the complete freedom of the soul and allowed it to escape to the domain of Pluto, god of the Underworld. To ensure him a comfortable last journey the dead man's tomb was filled with a few practical and precious objects such as vases, choice plate and jewelry. The human preoccupation with display had its place in this emergent funerary art, though stele and chapels were sometimes subject to restrictive laws. In the Hellenistic period, however, the taste of kings and princes for monumental architecture also found its expression in their tombs, and the fine mausoleum erected by Artemisia for her husband Mausolus became the prototype of a line which continued until the end of the Roman period. It extended over the western world, reaching Gaul and Spain by way of Sicily, where the tomb of Theron, set among the almond trees of Agrigento still serves as a reminder of its progress.

Ritual and religious festivals

Theoretically, sacrificial rites seemed to have been designed in accordance with a common formula consisting of the preparations, the actual sacrifice and the arrangements which followed it. In actual fact, however, the ritual was highly diversified depending on the personality of the divinity, his functions and the benefits expected from him.

The examples which follow are confined to rites which exercised some influence over the construction of buildings dedicated to the service of the divinity. Sacrifices offered to the gods of Olympus were celebrated on raised altars often, as at Priene and Pergamon, strikingly monumental in character. On the other hand, those destined for the divinities of the earth or the dead were placed on low altars with hollows in the center to allow the victims' blood to flow directly on to the ground. Some were celebrated in the presence of worshipers gathered on a vast esplanade, while other rites were more secret. The famous tholos at Epidaurus was probably a funerary altar.

Mysteries and oracles

The requirements of private rites brought about improvements in architectural design. The mystery cults, which were reserved for initiates, needed halls for the initiation ceremonies. Little is known of the ritual of the Eleusinian mysteries dedicated to Demeter and Persephone, but the sanctuary contains the most famous of these Telesteria where the worshipers witnessed plays evoking their advance towards divine revelations and supernatural life.

It was the duty of the oracular gods to answer worshipers' questions, to justify their actions and direct them to taking decisions most favorable to their private or public activities. To consult them, after a preliminary sacrifice, also involved a complex ritual. Zeus at Dodona and Apollo at Delphi, Clarus and Didyma used a variety of means to convey their answers.

At Dodona the prophet interpreted the calls of doves, the shakings of oak leaves and the deep echoes of a cauldron. The Pythia at Delphi and the prophets of Claros and Didyma found inspiration in drinking water from sacred springs and wells. They prophesied out of sight of the worshipers within the adyton, the plan of which survives at Claros and Didyma. The answers were relayed by skilled interpreters, either in prose or verse.

According to Strabo: 'The seat of the oracle is usually a cavern with a narrow opening hollowed out of the earth; from it emerges the breath of inspiration; above the opening is set a lofty tripod on to which the Pythia climbs; she receives the breath and delivers the oracle in verse and prose; they are also transcribed into verse by poets in the service of the sanctuary.'

An oracle of the dead or Necromanteion recently discovered in Epirus has an underground layout giving a clue to the complexities of the ceremonies ordained for the consultation of the dead, though this cannot be confirmed in any text.

Of the oracular rites which influence architecture, special mention must be made of the consultations of the divinities of healing, particularly Asclepius. With the aid of Aristophanes's comedy 'Plutus' and the inscribed monuments at Epidaurus, it is possible to follow the vicissitudes of the sick. After offering a preliminary sacrifice, they settled under the colonnades for a night's sleep during which the god or his servants visited them and either informed them of the means to a cure or effected one on the spot.

The ceremonials of the festivals held in honor of the gods were just as rich and complex. They included processions sometimes accompanied by the god's effigy, sacred banquets, songs and music and, in more important cases, a variety of gymnastic, literary and musical competitions. All these went to make up the panegyris which was accompanied by great popular gatherings combining political and commercial elements. The most famous games were those held at Olympia, Delphi, the sanctuary of the isthmus of Corinth, and Nemea, all of which were hymned by Pindar. Equally famous was the Panathenaea depicted by Phidias in the frieze round the shrine of the Parthenon. There were, however, countless similar festivals held throughout the city states in honor of humbler divinities. An inscription from Thasos sets out the festival calendar month by month as follows:

Month	Festivals	Divinities
October–November (Apaturion)	Apaturia Festival of all the gods	Zeus Patroos Athena Patroie
November–December (Maimakterion)	Maimakteria	Zeus
December–January (Poseideion)	Poseideia	Poseidon
February–March (Anthesterion)	Anthesteria Soteria	Dionysus Hercules Soter
March–April (Galaxion)	Dionysia	Dionysus
April–May (Artemesion)	Diasia	Zeus
May–June (Thargelion)	Great Herakleia Choreia	Hercules Dionysus
June–July (Plynterion)	Duodekatheria	The Twelve Gods
July–August	Alexandreia	Alexander the Great
(Hecatombaion)	Thesmophoria	Demeter and Persephone
August–September	Great Asclepieia	Asclepius
September–October	Demetrieia Heroxeinia Dioscuria Great Komara	Demeter The Heroes The Dioscuri Apollo Komaios

This was obviously a heavy program particularly in the last month of the year corresponding to our months of September and October. To this list must also be added all the festivals of the panhellenic sanctuaries in which the Greek city states took part and those of other cities to which they were invited and sent delegations. From this we may judge the place occupied by religious festivals in the lives of the Greeks, and the importance of the buildings devoted to them.

Intellectual and artistic life

It is impossible to ignore those aspects of intellectual and artistic life which exercised an influence on the architecture of ancient Greece. Both the great panhellenic festivals and those held in honor of a diversity of gods in every city and in small, isolated sanctuaries, included a literary or musical program. The public readings at Olympia in which Herodotus, Gorgias and Isocrates took part, the songs inspired by choral poetry, the musical competitions at the Panathenaea, and the theatrical performances held at Athens during the Great Dionysia and the Lenaea, all collected a vast and enthusiastic audience. The theater deserves particular mention both for the famous names which added to its luster and for the essential part it played in the life of the citizens. The Greeks were, and continue to be, a race devoted to the theater, and it was the custom in Athens to credit all poor citizens with the few obols needed to enable them to be present at all the performances of the great contests at which Aeschylus, Sophocles, Euripedes and Aristophanes in turn won their crowns. The Athenians crowded to performances and participated in them to the full. These competitive theatrical performances were religious, literary, and even political in character, and very soon theaters were accorded an important position in city plans. Along with the agora and the temples, the theater became a basic element in the city's architectural layout and played an essential part in the life of the community.

During the Hellenistic period, intellectual life developed against a better planned background. Schools of philosophy and academic teaching became associated with gymnasia, and, at Athens, some of these lent their names to the philosophical movements they sheltered. At Pergamon, Alexandria and Rhodes, libraries, assembly halls and porticoes were grouped together to form real academic centers. This period saw a development of theater design and its division into categories. Concert halls, odeia, and miniature theaters for lectures or public readings were established as part of the architectural layout of gymnasia and palaestra, and were erected on public squares or in small temples. In this way, the comprehensive broadening of artistic and intellectual life brought about original types of building.

Mention should also be made of the sanctuaries of the Muses or museia, some of the most delightful architectural creations associated with philosophy and literature. In the Hellenistic period these were set in valleys or gardens like the most famous of them all on Mount Helicon, near Thespiae. The altars of the goddesses were hidden in groves, there was a small theater and colonnade to protect the offerings. They provided havens of quiet for philosophers, artists and men of letters. They also formed some of the most typical architectural landscapes of the period and greatly influenced later garden architecture.

Plates

Aegosthena – Fort

21 4th century Boeotian fort. Square towers built of isodomic masonry with bulges. Long and short blocks alternate in each course. Two-storeyed tower.

22 General view of the fort on the shore of the Gulf of
/23 Corinth showing the regular alternation of curtain wall and towers, 15 of which are in a good state of preservation.

Eleutherae – Fort

24 4th century fort guarding the road from Attica to Boeotia. Masonry known as 'emplekton' consisting of two facings in regular courses enclosing a filling of rubble and earth. (Average thickness of curtain walls: 8.5 feet).

25 General view of curtain walls. Note the rebates at the corners and the trapezoidal shape of some of the blocks. The towers project on either side of the curtain wall.

Messene – Ramparts and Arcadian Gate

26 Ramparts of the lower town built at the period of its great expansion in the first half of the 4th century. The curtain walls climb the slopes and are defended by alternate round and square towers.

27 Detail of a door in one of the towers giving on to the wall-walk. Note the long headstones laid the full width of the curtain wall.

28 Detail of a circular tower with doors giving on to the wall-walk. The battlements and coping stones on its summit still survive. Eventually, some of the towers were roofed, sheltering the defenders from sling-bullets or flaming projectiles. This transformation resulted from progress made in ballistics.

29 Interior of a tower showing the way out to the wall-walk with a defensive parapet. On the right is a loop-hole allowing the defenders to aim their weapons at the foot of the curtain wall. Above may be seen a cavity to accommodate one of the beams supporting the floor of a room on the upper storey.

30 The Arcadian Gate situated on the north side of the town. Detail of a niche prepared for the effigy of a female divinity, protectress of gates.

31 General view of the circular court which acted as a defensive position in front of the gate. Fine masonry consisting at ground level of a course of orthostats surmounted by a low coping: above this are alternate blocks and headers. In the passage-way is the lintel of the outer gate.

32 Detail of the inner walls of the courtyard. Above the smooth course of orthostats and its coping, the faces of the blocks are marked with parallel striations cut with a pointed chisel. This decoration accentuates the plasticity of the masonry which is powerfully articulated by the horizontal chamfered joints.

Perga, Pamphylia – Hellenistic ramparts

33 Detail of a corner tower. The masonry consists of blocks, their faces ornamented with panels in relief surrounded by grooves. The projecting course corresponds with the floor of an upper room supplied with openings through which weapons could be fired.

34 Courtyard inside the gate outlined by a series of arcades supporting the wall-walk.

35 Detail of a pilaster supporting the springers of two of the arches. The capital has a plain outline and is made of a dark limestone more resistant than the soft stone of the walls and arches.

36 The great gate of the town. The passage-way is framed by two circular towers with bulging masonry, both highly decorative and, according to Philo, extremely useful for protecting the joints against sling-bullets. The wall-walk supported by the arcades was originally roofed.

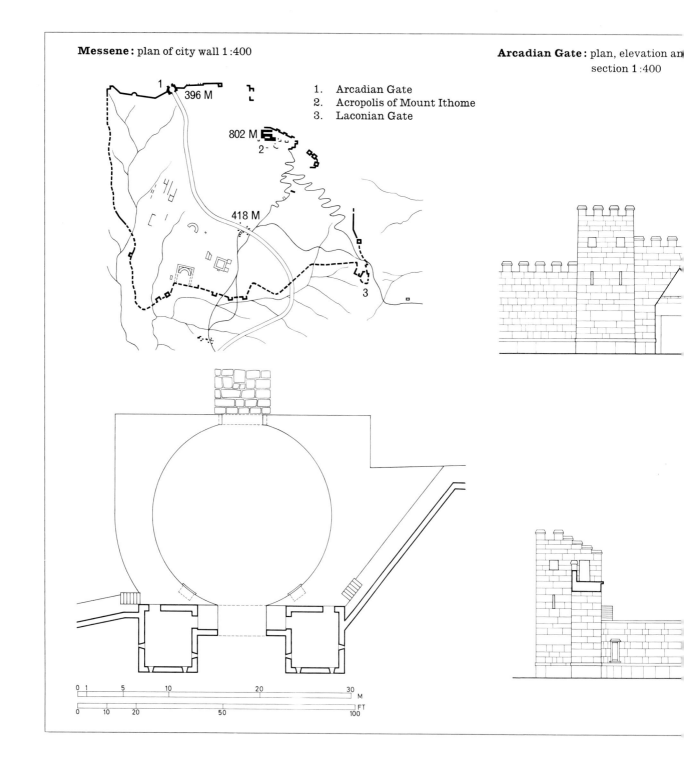

Messene: plan of city wall 1:400

396 M

1. Arcadian Gate
2. Acropolis of Mount Ithome
3. Laconian Gate

802 M

2-

418 M

3

Arcadian Gate: plan, elevation and section 1:400

0 1   5   10   20   30
                                                    M
0   10   20   50   100
                                                    FT

18

Perga main gate: elevation and plan 1:400

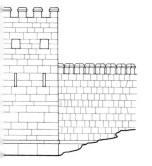

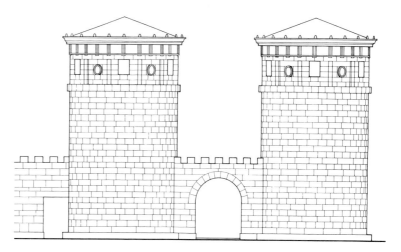

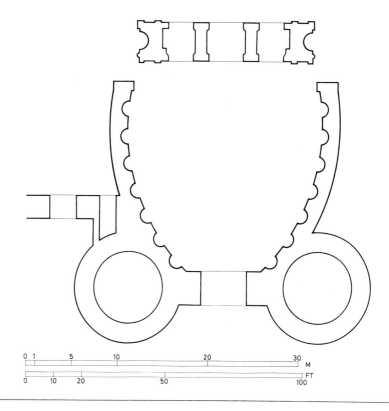

```
0  1      5        10              20              30
|__|_____|_____|_____|_____| M
0     10    20              50                    100
|_____|_____|_____|_____| FT
```

Notes

4th century forts – Attica and Boeotia

The foreign policies of the city states of the Greek mainland after the defeat of Athens, and the shifting series of alliances which helped to keep a balance between Athens, Thebes, Sparta and, later, Macedonia led, over this period, to the building of frontier forts at a distance from the towns to defend the border passes and protect crossing points. Phyle and Rhamnus in Attica, Eleutherae and Aegosthena in Boeotia are the best examples of these forts, and most evocative of the military policies of the fourth-century city states. They also bear witness to the development of military establishments. In Attica, the regulations ordained that young Athenians should pass the second year of their initiation into manhood serving as garrison troops in these forts. Henceforward, these structures were no longer merely provisional defence points but the seats of permanent garrisons with an organizational system and a life of their own, as can be discovered from surviving documents relating to Rhamnus. This explains their architectural style: strong walls and many well-ordered towers surrounding a group of military and civil buildings which provided the garrison with a setting for a carefully organized mode of life under the direct authority of the commandant, himself responsible to the state assembly. The carefully worked out constructional technique was based on the use of large blocks set in regular courses, and was dictated by functional needs. The curtain walls, whose thickness varied from 5.9 feet to 10 feet, were adapted to the lie of the land, occupying commanding positions. No use was made, however, of artificial slopes and ditches. The wall-walks and towers of the earliest forts were unroofed and it was not until the end of the century that inscriptions regarding repairs to the walls at Athens referred to the systematic provision of roofs. The walls were composed of two outer facings made up of large blocks with a filling of marble in between. Low transverse walls or headers ensured a link between the facings. This was the technique known as 'emplekton.' The facings were set in regular courses of more or less identical height. A decorative effect was obtained by the slender jointing; this sometimes deviated from the vertical, hence the name of trapezoidal masonry given to this constructional method. Plugs were very seldom used.

Messene

Though the fortifications of Messene also originated from the foreign policies and rivalries of the great city states of the 4th century, they fulfilled a different function. Epaminondas of Thebes in Boeotia, one of the best strategists of the 4th century, was well aware of the part that could be played by his city with its growing power and resolved to defeat Sparta on her own territory. Therefore, on receiving an appeal from the Arcadians, he advanced his army in the course of a few weeks as far as the banks of the Eurotas. Once there, he hesitated to take the city of Sparta by storm but determined to win a political and diplomatic victory over the Spartans on their own soil. To this end he set himself up as the defender of the principle of autonomy to which the Spartans had always outwardly subscribed and proclaimed the independence of Messenia which had for two hundred years been subject to Spartan domination. At the foot of the ancient citadel of Ithome, he created a new capital, Messene, surrounding it with a magnificent wall, a masterpiece of military architecture. Nearly 3.7 miles long it enclosed an area far in excess of that of the town. Thus it formed a place of refuge capable of accommodating the entire population of the region and of resisting the longest siege periods, both factors contrary to the customary tactics practised by the Spartans. In fact, it represented a severe blow directed against their sovereignty.

Perga and the towns of Pamphylia

In the Hellenistic period a splendid array of towns sprang up on the fertile plain between the Taurus range and the south coast of Anatolia, and their embellishment continued under the Roman occupation. All were built on magnificent sites and each had a citadel dominating a lower town with its own fortifications. Inspired by examples of town planning on the west coast, especially at Pergamon, and, in some cases, coming within the sphere of influence of the Attalids, they presented a monumental scale and architectural invention unsurpassed elsewhere. The magnificent gate reproduced here is a fine example. The outer approach is framed by the restrained yet powerful masonry of two great towers. It leads into a vast open space which serves to increase the proportions of the inner gates and is lent well defined rhythm by the succession of arcaded niches forming its boundary.

Perga, tower of city wall: elevation and plan 1:200   Arcades of city wall: elevation, plan and section 1:200

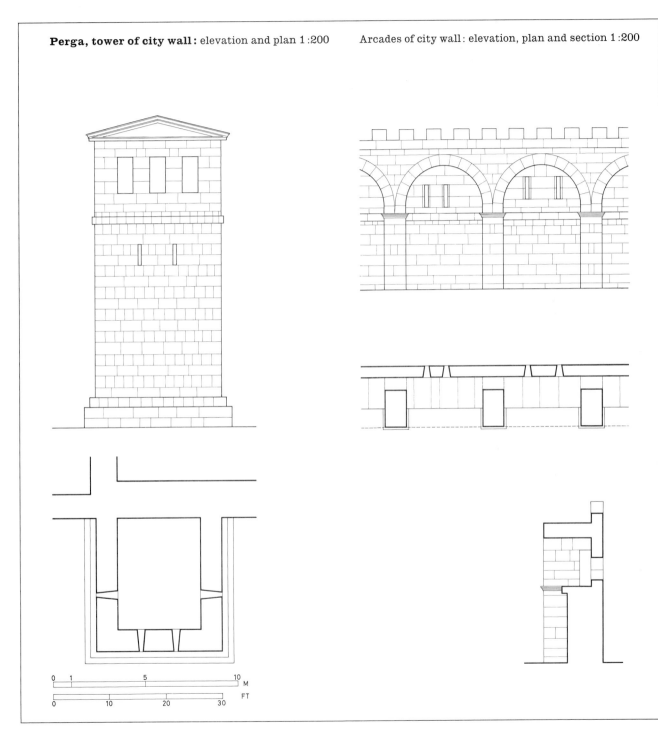

0 1   5   10   M

0   10   20   30   FT

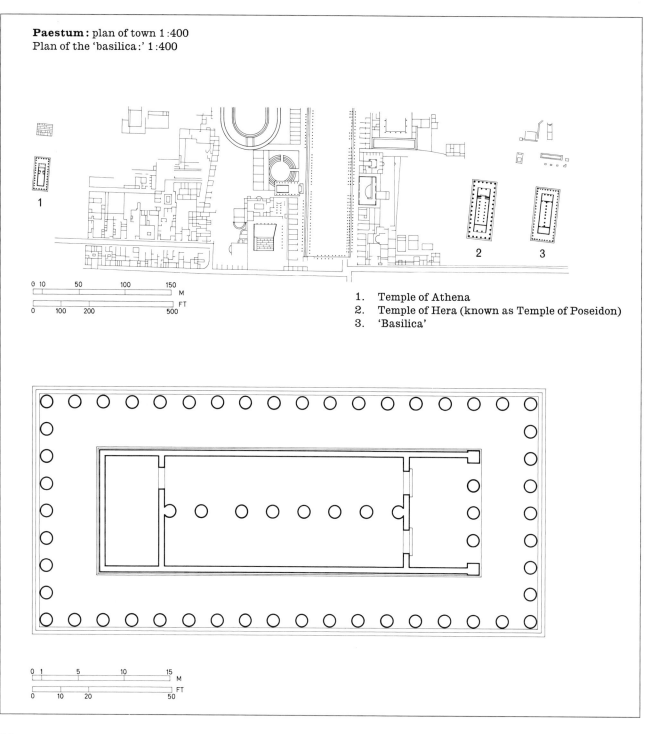

Paestum: plan of town 1:400
Plan of the 'basilica:' 1:400

0 10   50   100   150
                             M
0   100   200   500
                          FT

1. Temple of Athena
2. Temple of Hera (known as Temple of Poseidon)
3. 'Basilica'

0 1   5   10   15
                         M
0   10   20   50
                        FT

2. Practicalities of Building

Patrons and programs

Explanation of the preponderance of official commissions over private enterprise in Greek architecture lies in the historical and religious background against which it developed. Except in the late Hellenistic period, in outlying regions or in the colonies, patrons were seldom private individuals. Even when a private citizen devoted his own resources to a work of architecture, he did so on behalf of his city for its sole advantage. Only the dedicatory inscription indicated the personal nature of the commission.

Thus the city states themselves headed the list of patrons, their chief duty being to the gods and their temples, then to public and administrative buildings. They were followed by the administrators of the great sanctuaries who were responsible for providing worshipers with temples and buildings required for both religious and secular functions, such as porticoes and guest houses. On the other hand, the adornment of the great sanctuaries was to a great extent provided by the individual city states which vied with one another in the provision of costly treasuries, porticoes and fountains. Olympia, Delphi and Delos benefited most from this form of architectural diplomacy. When the monetary resources and political preponderance of the city states diminished after the 4th century, it was the princes who came to the rescue, and the foundations of the kings of Macedon, the Attalids and the Ptolemies carried on the tradition of developing the architectural backgrounds of the sanctuaries. The Hellenistic kings and dynasts became the chief patrons and attracted the great Hellenistic architects to their courts. At the same time there was a considerable increase in the part played by private patrons owing to the heightened taste for huge, luxurious houses. Palaces were built which needed the services of decorators and painters as well as architects. The vast private

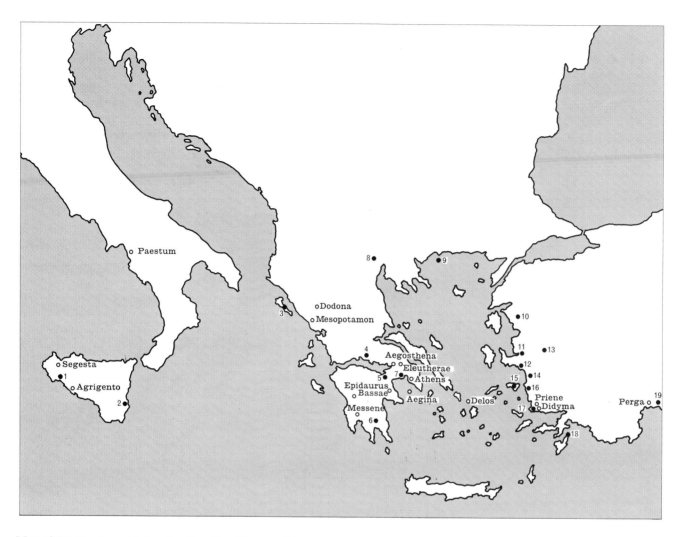

Map of the Greek world showing the sites illustrated in
the plates and the chief places mentioned in the text

1.	Selinunte	5.	Corinth	9.	Thasos	13.	Sardeis	17.	Halicarnassus
2.	Syracuse	6.	Sparta	10.	Pergamon	14.	Ephesus	18.	Rhodes
3.	Corfu	7.	Eleusis	11.	Smyrna	15.	Samos	19.	Side
4.	Delphi	8.	Pella	12.	Clarus	16.	Miletus		

houses of the royal capitals, the great trade centers and prosperous ports provided a new sphere of work for architects who entered into contracts with wealthy merchants. In this way there was a radical difference between the classical and Hellenistic periods.

This also resulted in important changes in methods of finance and administration. Most cities had magistrates chosen by the people and responsible for the funds put at their disposal. They saw to the maintenance of buildings, restoration work, the erection of small structures, the police force and the application of town-planning regulations. As far as Athens was concerned there are textual references to a superintendent of religious buildings, a college responsible for the maintenance of the ramparts to which Demosthenes belonged, an architect responsible for the sanctuary of Demeter at Eleusis, and a group of technicians who saw to the repair of streets and roads. There is also evidence of an organized service of architects in several towns, usually consisting of two or three elected on a permanent basis by the people for the purpose of seeing to repair work, enforcing the local regulations, erecting commemorative monuments, etc. In other words they fulfilled all the functions of a municipal architect's department. Their special task was to carry out the official town plan.

Sketch of the Arsenal at the Piraeus, according to the specification

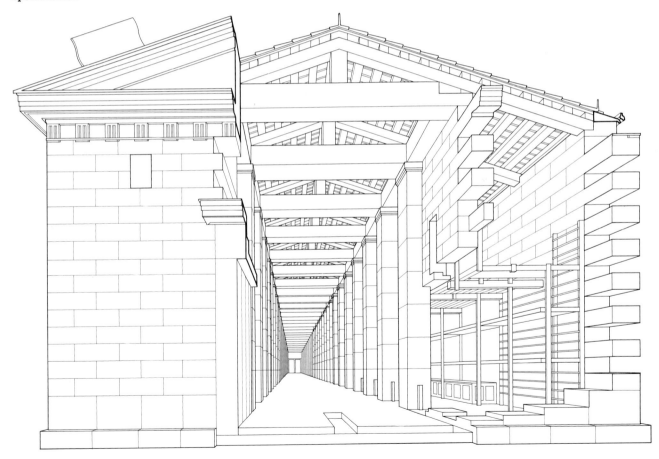

In the case of very important architectural programs, such as the erection of temples, ramparts or administrative or commercial buildings, decisions were arrived at by a vote of the popular assembly after a proposal by the council which made its choice from a model. The decree voted by the assembly set up a commission composed of several members; they were, in fact, the real organizers of the work, being responsible for the preparation and execution of the program. A competition was declared open regarding the program drawn up by the council and ratified by the assembly, for which architects had to submit estimates and projects.

Here again contemporary texts shed light on the detailed requirements of the administrative ordinances to which architects and contractors were strictly subjected. Among them are the regulations regarding the nature of the arsenal built at the Piraeus by Philo. The measurements quoted in the following extract belong to the Attic system according to which the plethron equalled 100 feet, or more precisely 97.7 feet. The foot was again divided into 16 dactyles, or 4 palms:

'Conditions for the stone arsenal designed for the rigging [of boats], [constructed] by Euthydimus, son of Demetrius of Miletus, and Philo, son of Execates of Eleusis . . . the building to begin from the propylon of the agora. For the part stretching towards the propylon starting from the rear of the slipways with which it will have a common roof, the length will be 4 plethra, the width 15 feet, including the walls. [The foundations] will be dug to a depth of 3 feet from the highest point, the remainder having been levelled; the bulk of the foundations will be set on the firm soil and the courses will be raised to a uniform height; the whole to be made level . . . The walls and pillars of the arsenal will be built of stone and the walls will be set on a base . . . The walls will be built of blocks 4 feet long and

$5\frac{1}{2}$ feet wide. At each corner the length of the blocks will be regulated according to the measurements of the triglyphs. The wall above the base will be given a height of 27 feet including the triglyph below the cornice . . . There will be windows all round in all the walls, one in the space between each pillar and, in the side walls, three on each side. Height: 3 feet; width: 2 feet.'

When, in the 4th century, the Athenians wished to carry out important restoration work on the city walls and the Long Walls which protected the road linking the city with the Piraeus, the regulations were just as detailed. Each section was placed in the care of an assistant architect whose responsibility was to oversee and control the contractors working on it. After reference to the architect's specifications and proposals governed by the building committee, the regulations pass to more detailed estimates. Equipment, the delivery and transport of materials, the hewing and positioning of stone are sometimes the subject of overall estimates, but more often are accounted for separately. The same contractor could only be responsible for one or two sections and sureties had to be provided. These precautionary measures were due to the fact that the contractors' financial resources were limited. Moreover, the methods of payment did not allow them much scope; the account was rendered in three parts – half midway through the work and half, less a fraction usually amounting to one tenth, after the completion and formal reception of the building. The remainder was settled after a period of verification including definite reception by the architect and the consent of the committee. The texts reveal the tight restrictions imposed on architects and contractors. A set of rules from Tegea defines the legal aspects of conflicts which could arise between architects and contractors. They contain the following administrative clauses:

– Institution of a special court (the tribunal of adjudicators for all questions relating to the work) (1.1.);
– arrangements relating to cases where the works might be interrupted by a war (1.6.);
– measures to be taken in case of obstacles being put in the way of the adjudications (1.15.);
– prohibition of being responsible for more than two simultaneous undertakings without special authorization (1.20.);
– interdiction of any action before extraneous tribunals (1.30.).

Function of the architect

The restrictions applied to architects were not only of a financial nature. They also arose from the confined scope of the projects and, still more often, resulted from local traditions, religious strictures attached to the site and regulations applied to previous buildings. The plans of earlier buildings had to be respected and the old materials which were frequently reused for reasons of economy could impose their pattern and proportions. Ictinus, the architect of the Parthenon, had to take into account the foundations and dimensions of the columns of the unfinished temple which had already been started on the site. The sculptor Phidias who required an interior worthy of his projected statue of the goddess Athene was, in fact, the real master architect of the Acropolis. Complex regulations governed the possession of holy ground, and the sites of the various divinities associated with the sanctuary imposed many restrictions. Mnesicles, too, was caught between the plans of earlier buildings on the Acropolis, in particular the propylon of Peisistratus, respect for traditional rights and reserved zones, and the demands of a difficult site; thus, he had to exert considerable imagination and evolve subtle solutions for the placing of his monumental Propylaea.

We would like to have more exact knowledge of the working conditions enjoyed by these architects who had to submit to so many curbs. These alone can allow us to grasp the creative possibilities available to them and their basic originality. Our aesthetic judgment of Greek architecture must, in the final resort, depend on this.

The fundamental evidence lies in their highly detailed descriptive specifications. In actual fact, Greek architects do not seem to have made numerous preparatory sketches to illustrate their projects. They submitted their work for the approval of the bodies appointed by the state in the form of maquettes and the actual work was also carried out in accordance with similar models made of wood or terracotta. Details such as capitals, gutter moldings and corner blocks were also executed after models supplied by the architect. Some ocher drawings on whitened panels were made to illustrate the preparation of specially shaped blocks for the entablature and other features, but ordinary blocks were quarried and hewn in accordance with the proportions quoted in the descriptive specification. The architect took charge of the receipt of materials from the quarry and checked them with his figures and models; sometimes blocks were refused entrance to the workshop and returned to the quarriers. The actual hewing and placing of the blocks did not involve strict precision. A wide margin was left to the executant in the way of detail which accounts for the amount of reworking and other transformations effected on buildings in course of construction, and the important part played by workshop traditions and regional customs.

Thus, the architects' originality was often limited to the choice of order – though here, too, regional influences carried great weight – to adopting a traditional plan to the ritualistic and topographical requirements of the site, in which respect they were guided by a sure sense for the relationship between building and landscape, to the design of the details of the order and the working out of its proportions, and the choice of decorative elements if there was no associated sculptor. Nevertheless, in an architecture based on simple forms of construction and strict geometrical lines, a high standard of preparation and placing of materials were factors of prime importance and constitute two of the great attainments of the Greek builders. With their methods and conditions of execution, this was largely due to the skill of the workmen, masons and stonecutters. It is essential to bear this in mind when passing artistic judgment on Greek architecture.

Workshops

We must consider what knowledge we have of these humble craftsmen and their life in the workshops. Texts relating to buildings at Athens, Delos, Delphi and Epidaurus help to throw some light on their working methods and conditions and their way of life. Their technique is best studied later in relation to their buildings. First, we should try to find out what sort of people they were. Citizens, foreigners and slaves were all employed together in the workshops. The teams that labored to complete the Erechtheum included a few Athenians but a larger number of foreigners and slaves. The great temple of Apollo at Didyma was built by large contingents of slaves belonging either to the god, the town of Miletus, or local contractors. The contractors were usually citizens, but, both at Delos and Athens, a great number of the timber suppliers were foreigners from Syria and Asia Minor.

The specialized workers were very often connected with materials with which they were familiar. At Epidaurus, the contractors and workmen from Argos and Corinth provided and worked on tufa and limestone from the Peloponnese, while the Athenians were responsible for the delivery and cutting of the Pentelic marble used to build the tholos. At Delphi, teams from the Peloponnese worked on the temple of Apollo which was built of tufa, but the treasuries were constructed by marble-workers from the islands. Later on, the consignments of marble to the Roman towns of Cyrenaica were accompanied by Attic craftsmen who left their signatures on the pieces for which they were responsible. These temporary migrations of craftsmen who accompanied their local materials influenced and transformed the working methods of individual regions.

We must now consider their working conditions. The erection of a large building necessitated the opening of a permanent workshop. A studio also had to be constructed to shelter stonecutters preparing moldings, sculptors responsible for the figured decoration, and craftsmen preparing doors ornamented with ivory and bronze. All involved worked under the supervizion of a foreman who was directed by the architect and responsible for the standard of the work. Judging from the accounts for the Erechtheum, salaries were fixed by agreement. There was a rate for a specific piece of work such as the fluting of columns, and a day rate for specialists. Workers, both slaves and free citizens, were formed into squads, and their foreman saw to the payments; they alone are mentioned by name in the accounts.

Besides their salaries the workers were entitled to allowances for food and clothing. Sometimes, however, as with the category defined by Athenaeus as 'workers who labor for their food alone,' this was their only salary. Some 3rd century building accounts referring to Delos show that there was, in fact, a canteen for the benefit of the members of the workshop. An allowance of 10 drachmas per man per month was paid out for provisions; fixed quantities of flour, wheat and barley, paid for out of the temple coffers, were handed over to a baker to ensure a supply of bread for the workers. A clothing allowance is also mentioned.

Architects were entitled to travel allowances when, as at Epidaurus, they did not live on the site, but visited it regularly; at Delos they received an accommodation allowance which was added to their current salary. The architects who are mentioned regularly in the Delos accounts as supervizing the workshops and checking the work, were employed by the temple officials and were technicians paid in the same way as the contractors and workmen. Good contractors could also be awarded the title and fixed salary of an architect. Official architects employed by the city states operated in Athens and many other towns; they were responsible for the maintenance of public buildings and could remain in office for several years. When it was a question of important architectural works, however, an architect was specially chosen by vote.

The successive architects who supervized the building of the temple of Apollo at Delphi after 373 B.C. were probably similar to the salaried architect-contractors of Delos; their salaries did not exceed those of the stonecutters. A Delos account dating from the late 4th century records that, in addition to an exceptionally high salary, the architect received an accommodation allowance of 120 drachmas. The large salary together with this exceptional payment suggest that a a more highly qualified architect had been engaged on a different level from the civil servants employed by the temple officials for ordinary work. All these factors make us vary our aesthetic judgments and bear in mind under what conditions the great buildings of Greece were erected. There were several causes for the variable uncertainties of some of these buildings, including the modest payment of the workers, the strict controls exerted by city states and temple authorities, the continual supervision of those responsible for the building work, and the small numbers of the well trained labor force.

Costs

The subject of costs was of prime importance in all periods of architecture. A building account from Eleusis dating from 329-8 B.C. mentions that the price of stones for a retaining wall was 3 drachmas, 1 obol per stone. The price included the quarrying, transport and laying in position. Another passage from the same text provides all details relating to a consignment of paving stones; price of quarrying each block, 1 drachma, 1 obol. Transport: 1 drachma, 3 obols. Placing in position, 1 drachma, the last being the cheapest item. In the case of the Erechtheum, about 405 B.C., the price for laying varied according to the length of the blocks, varying from 10 drachmas for blocks 8 feet long to 2 drachmas 3 obols and 2 drachmas 4 obols for 3 and 4 feet blocks. Prices were higher at Didyma in the 3rd century, the cost of a cubic foot being one drachma, whereas, at the Erechtheum, it was never more than 4 obols.

The setting up of a column involved more work. The cost of quarrying and transport of tufa for each column of the hypostyle stoa at Delos was fixed at 185 drachmas and the erection of a column came to 49 drachmas in one case, 54 in another. This represented a little less than a third of the price of the whole; a similar proportion of costs may also be found in the accounts for Eleusis.

An examination of the cost of the great columns of the temple of Apollo at Didyma reveals similar findings. The temple accounts offer a fairly exact reckoning of the main expenses incurred in the erection of columns. The cost, according to those responsible, seems to have been as much as 38.787 drachmas.

This was split up into three more or less equal parts: extraction and preparation at the quarry, 13.151 drachmas; expenses of sea and overland transport including the journeys from the quarry at Maratha to Ionopolis, the port of embarkation, and from Panormus, the port of landing, to the temple workshop, 12.938 drachmas; finally, setting up of the various sections and sculptures, scraping and fluting of the shafts, 12.698 drachmas. This last item was particularly expensive for the type of column found at Didyma but, even so, it did not exceed the cost of transport. Transport expenses were however, always very high on all sites. This explains the more usual employment of local materials and the frequent avoidance of rare, foreign marbles until the late Hellenistic period. The use of polychrome materials was favored for aesthetic reasons, but was often practised on a limited scale during the 5th and 4th centuries for reasons of economy.

Constructional methods and technique

References to supply, architects' accounts and notes on buildings all cohere and enable us to follow exactly the various stages in the construction of a building and the technical means of execution. Basic knowledge of these is an essential preliminary to the formation of aesthetic judgments.

Provision of materials

The first stage in any constructional undertaking was the provision of materials. Partners in the workshop supplied it directly with bricks, tiles and timber for framework and doorcases. Marble and stone, on the other hand, were secured by outside contract along with all other aspects of the operation. Bricks, tiles and timber were purchased directly by the cities or temples responsible for the building, and placed

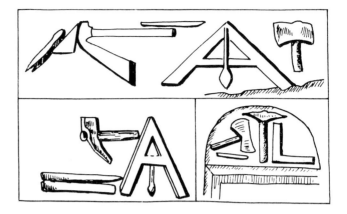

Stonecutter's equipment

in depots from which they could be withdrawn as needed. The amounts in these stores were checked annually by the temple officials at Delos along with the inventories of sacred treasures.

Orders passed to the quarries included all details relating to the building plan and the destination of each piece. Exact measurements and a sketch were provided by the architect and the blocks were extracted and cut to suit these requirements.

Pick and quarrying tool

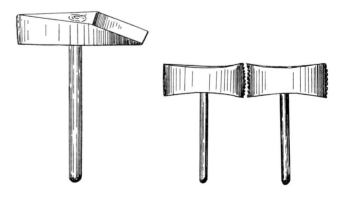

The architect exercised preliminary control at the quarry and the final acceptance of the block took place after delivery to the stone-yard. If the terms of the contract were not fulfilled, the block could be returned to the quarry as is known to have happened at Eleusis and Didyma. To allow such checks, and as proof of payments, blocks bore painted or carved marks which have in some cases survived. These simple signs consisted of a few letters or complete names, providing references for those responsible. Little is known regarding the ordering of the quarries by the Greeks, but working methods under the Romans are more clearly documented.

In the Republican era quarries were owned by private individuals and by cities. Those at

Transport of blocks in Sicily

Reconstruction of trollies devized for the transport of lintels and architraves at Eleusis

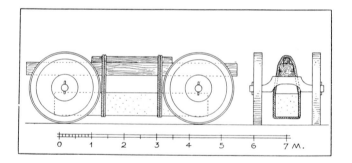

System of transporting blocks at Ephesus

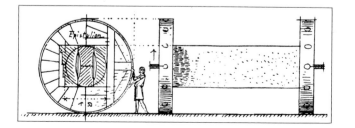

Synnada in Asia Minor still belonged in the early days of the Empire to a private individual, Marcus Agrippa, the minister of Augustus, and, in the 2nd century A.D. the Pentelic quarries were owned by Herod Atticus.

Quarries could be worked directly either by the owners or by contractors to whom they were leased. Under the Republic, mines and quarries belonging to the state were not worked directly but were let out to financial groups. After the establishment of the Empire, the imperial quarries were apparently under the direct management of the Emperor's civil service and their working was the charge of his procurator. The labor was directed by foremen acting under his orders and carried out by freemen, slaves and convicts.

After the blocks had been delivered and received by the workshop, they passed to the stonecutters to be made more suitable to fulfil their function and to assume their final shape. This work was carried out in accordance with the sketches and models provided by the architect. The sheaths designed for protection during transport were partly removed, but care was taken to fix pads to the corners by means of knobs so as to prevent undue scraping during the setting up. Projecting tenons were also left to enable cords to be fixed for hoisting, and cavities were prepared to accommodate levers. The inventory of blocks prepared but still not set up in the temporarily abandoned workshops of the Erechtheum shows that only some of the joints were made ready. Only the lower surface and the lateral joints which would come in contact with blocks already in position were smoothed and polished. The others were still rough and were only finished off when they had been manoeuvred into place. Similarly surfaces that were to receive moldings or sculptured friezes were left marked out and the drums of columns remained without their fluting. This type of work was done after the positioning.

Thus, preparation in the workshop amounted to no more than the completion of the shaping begun in the quarry.

Setting up

The setting up and assembly of blocks was a specially important operation in an architecture which rejected the use of mortar or plaster, except in the case of country buildings made of rubble, and only relied on accurate joints or links in the form of metal bolts and seals. It resorted to the piling up of courses which were held in place by gravity alone. There was no need to have recourse to buttresses except occasionally to break vertical facings which were too massive or subjected to the outward thrust of terraces above. It was enough to prevent blocks from slipping over one another or gaps from appearing between the carefully calculated joints. This was the function of metal seals and bands which seem to have had limited powers of resistance in comparison with the massive weights they had to support.

Sometimes these weights were considerable, as in the great temples whose marbled architraves 10 or 13 feet long or sometimes more, had to be set above columns 33 or 39 feet high. The widespread theory that the Greeks used inclined planes after the fashion of the Egyptians may, however, be dismissed. This originated from a passage in the Elder Pliny's 'Natural History' (XXXVI, 14). It is highly unlikely that such a device would have been needed on the threshold of the 6th century by an engineer architect of the caliber of Theodorus of Samos who strove to secure the foundations of the temple in the marshy soil. On the other hand, it is possible that Cherisiphron and Metagenes experienced some difficulty in setting a marble architrave 28.5 feet long and over 20 tons in weight above columns more than 40 feet high, and that they resorted to exceptional measures suggested by Theodorus after he had paid a visit to Egypt.

Such baseless stories were inspired by the

Method of lifting with double pincers and U-shaped grooves

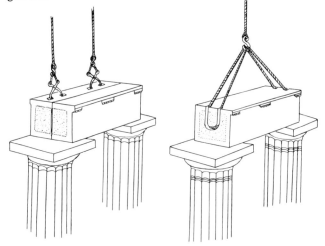

48

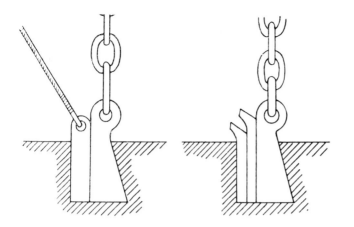

Two types of sling with a single oblique surface

vast buildings on the coast of Asia Minor which baffled the Greeks from the mainland accustomed to the more restricted proportions of the architecture of their ancient cities. It is unlikely, however, that such procedures were ever current in Greece, especially as signs of hoists used in the workshops may be found on blocks dating from the early 6th century. These first took the form of wide U-shaped grooves cut in the end faces of the blocks, and then of V-shaped cavities set on the upper surface. Finally, there were tenons projecting from the facing, some of which still survive. All these devices were designed to facilitate the passing of ropes and slings needed to raise the blocks. The late 6th and 5th centuries saw the development of cavities to act as fastenings for the great hooks used by the quarrymen and, finally, came mortices designed to control the slings. All great Greek buildings were erected with the aid of these devices involving the use of winches, pulleys and blocks, all of which would have been familiar to a sea-going people.

The blocks prepared on the site were set up course by course in the walls. Two teams often worked together, each starting from one end of the wall so that the course was completed by the placing in the center of the last block which held all the others in position. Each block was deposited by the machines on the course below and was brought to its final resting place with the help of rollers and crowbars. The position and shape of the notches are valuable indications of the method and order of construction.

Once the course was complete its upper surface was hewn and polished to receive the next. Then, cavities were chiselled out for bolts and plugs. The pegs and tenons of wood, bronze or iron were finally coated with molten lead which filled any gaps and prevented the infiltration of water. For it was imperative to prevent oxidization, which could split the marble. This was encountered in the course of the early restorations of the buildings on the Acropolis at Athens when, after some unfortunate experiments, it was found necessary to have recourse to the methods of the original builders.

Tripod with hoisting gear

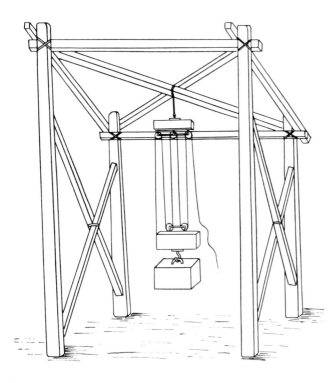

Tetrakolos – hoisting gear with pulley blocks

channel hollowed out on the upper surface of the drum. This was done with the help of an earthenware crucible which preserved the temperature necessary to keep the lead molten.

Types of bolt varied in accordance with the materials used and with regional tradition; they also provide evidence for dating. The oldest ones were dovetailed; the earliest ones contained a piece of wood or bronze of identical shape, the later ones a right-angled clamp with small hooks. In the classic period all the buildings of Attica had bolts with T-shaped projections and, from the 4th century until the end of the antique period there was general use of simple right-angled clamps curved at both ends and fixed in a cavity with two parallel sides.

The workmen whose task was to set up and assemble the blocks had only models or rough sketches which allowed a fair degree of liberty

Setting up wall blocks with the aid of crowbars

The same principles held good for the construction of columns. The drums were prepared on the site beneath a light protective covering. The lower surfaces were polished over a restricted area to facilitate the jointing and the central portions were hollowed out and pegged. Bolts were fixed ready for engaging in the corresponding mortices set on the upper surface of the drum already in position. This surface was only prepared after the section had been erected. The bolts, made of wood or bronze, were cylindrical or quadrangular in shape and embedded in a shallow bowl of the same substance attached to the mortice. This precise and delicate work was made easier in the Hellenistic period by the freer play allowed to the bowl whose chinks were covered with a coating of molten lead. The lead was brought to the center of the column by a

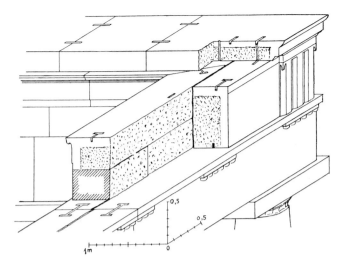

Fastening blocks with clamps

based on established techniques and also left room for a certain amount of invention; thus, to avoid mistakes, they had to be guided by fairly exact indicating marks. These were found on the blocks and on various sections of the building as the construction work gradually advanced. The architect ensured that the courses, the blocks of each course and the drums of the columns were numbered. When the podium of a temple was prepared to receive the walls and columns, carved marks outlined the walls and indicated the exact positions of the columns. At each level other marks delineated the projection of one course over another or the boundary of the frieze and architrave. At Didyma, the marks defining the spacing of the fluting on the columns were accompanied by numbers which allowed the craftsmen to follow the decrease in diameter. Sometimes, as in the Laphrion at Calydon, abbreviations indicated the setting of the blocks or fixed their positions in relation to the façade of the building, as in the temple of Ares at Athens. This enables us to grasp the practical aspects of the builders' work and the strict watch kept over the details of each con-

structional stage by the architect or contractor.

Thus, it is clear that one of the chief attainments of Hellenic architecture lay in the high quality of its finished execution rather than in

Assembly marks on the rough-cast work at the Ionic temple, Pergamon

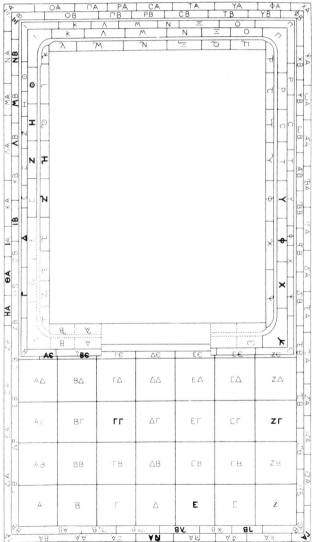

51

originality or feeling for composition. There was little development in the Greek temple plan throughout its history and it was repeated, with variations of detail, almost identically throughout the various regions of the Mediterranean world. On the other hand, the desire to perfect the execution of the simplest program coupled with rigid control of the application of traditional technical rules and a technique firmly based on materials used so as to set them off to best advantage, ensured that the completed work drew its perfection from the direct agreement established between the architect and his craftsmen.

This deep sensitivity towards materials and the constant desire to avoid working against them are revealed in the origins and development of mural decoration.

Here the aesthetic side was identical with the nature of the material used and the techniques of stone-cutting. The shape and construction of the jointing was of prime importance, followed by the type and application of facing. Fortifications, town ramparts, and retaining walls offered many variations. There were the supple, flexible outlines of so-called polygonal masonry where the blocks were carefully assembled with joints on several sides. Each block was cut with a view to its destined position and its contours were determined with the help of a lead gauge.

This form of masonry had the advantage of being very economical where materials were concerned but it required both skill and time. In the archaic period masonry became more regular and blocks with four jointed faces were preferred to polygonal shapes. There was, however, a transitional phase of trapezoidal masonry where the blocks maintained moderate independence of shape and height before the final adoption of rectangular blocks. These were quite regular and were assembled in courses with horizontal

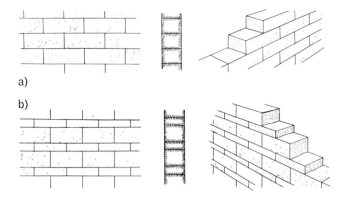

Masonry with binding stones:
a) isodomic;   b) pseudo-isodomic

joints. Their height could vary from one course to the next but remained constant in the same course.

In both these types of masonry particular attention was often paid to the jointing; the edges were beveled and worked with a sharp chisel, thus allowing the play of light on the face of the wall.

This, too, was skilfully treated by the stone-cutter. Polygonal masonry was usually combined with a slightly projecting wall face worked with a hammer; this presented a rough, splintered surface accentuating the interplay of light and shade. Masonry set in horizontal courses resulted in an increased effect of strength, especially in ramparts, on account of the highly rusticated surface. Skilfully executed with a pick or hammer, these walls looked like natural constructions.

The walls of buildings were similarly treated. In the classic period religious and secular buildings usually presented wide expanses of bare wall with smooth surfaces; paneled decoration appeared towards the end of the 5th century, the forerunner of countless effects subsequently deriving from it. The joints were surrounded by a groove which resulted in the projection of a slightly raised panel; this was sometimes emphasized by a slender frame surrounded by a chiseled scroll. Here again it was a case of bringing the wall to life, of attracting shadow and setting off the qualities of fine materials such as marble and limestone by skilful carving.

When the material did not merit such treatment, stucco made from powdered marble was

Masonry with square blocks and binders:
a) isodomic;   b) pseudo-isodomic

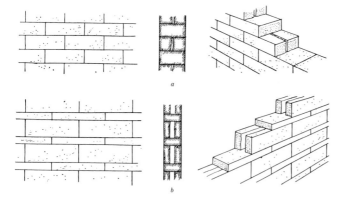

Masonry with square blocks and binders: variants

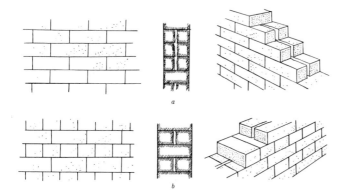

used as a special decorative facing. Some forms of limestone including coarse-grained tufa and conglomerates, usually reserved for foundations, did not permit choice carving. In these cases the decoration could be modeled in stucco, as occurs in the fluting of certain columns.

The citizens of Athens had neither the means nor the inclination to build themselves houses of marble. The lower walls were constructed of rubble, the upper ones of hollow bricks and humble materials were coated with mortar and plaster with a base of lime and sand. Yet the Greeks' feeling for architecture was expressed even in the decoration of these coatings. They were painted in a series of zones with strips of color separated by joints imitative of the block construction of an architectural wall. A dark colored plinth served as a base for large panels treated as uprights and a course decorated with painted moldings, heart- or egg-shaped, assured the transition to the upper sections which were treated as paneled masonry. This type of mural decoration originated at Olynthus in the 4th century and later spread to Priene and Delos.

Finishing

Smoothing and polishing constituted the final phase of construction. Numerous precautions were taken in the course of erection against possible forms of damage to the material, the quality of which formed an essential feature of the beauty of the completed building. The steps of the podium were provided with protective coverings and were also sheathed in wood or brick to allow the passage of columns and blocks for the outer walls. The lower parts of walls exhibiting decorative moldings were similarly protected, as in the Tholos at Epidaurus, the temple at Didyma and most Ionic buildings. Columns were set up without their flutings which were started from the base or sometimes on the last drum; there were carved or painted marks to guide the sculptors. Paving blocks were left rough with simple markings and the blocks for the courses had protective panels and projecting scrolls to guard their edges. All directions for the final smoothing were visible, carved in the stone; delicately marked bands outlined the surfaces to be worked on and marked out the project. A skilful arrangement of lines and flat moldings determined the limits of the planes and levels to which every surface had to comply. Moldings and decorative motifs were drawn by rule and measure.

An impression of strength emanates from the raw-looking materials, due to the powerful contrast between surfaces smoothed by chiseling and polishing and the rough, projecting ones which they frame. It is this which amplifies the plastic quality of Greek monumental architecture; it is possible to feel buildings progressively emerge from transformed materials.

Finishing off began with the smoothing of walls and polishing of surfaces in accordance with the directions of the architect, who had worked out the slope which allowed the large vertical planes to incline lightly towards the interior axes. Sometimes, as with the buildings of the Acropolis at Athens, the walls were treated as vast plane surfaces with no joints showing; panels taking up an entire wall were framed by hollow bands, as in the Propylaea of Mnesicles. In other cases, however, the joints were marked out with a chisel so that the wall surface was enlivened by a geometrical arabesque. Moldings were left in the rough with the designs outlined by compass. Gradually they were chiseled out and rounded curves emerged on the flat surfaces which began to disappear as these outlines took full shape. Simultaneously scaffolding was erected round the columns so that the fluting could be carried out; the cutting was done in two stages. The outline of the fluting

was sketched according to marks, some of which are still legible on the unfinished columns at Didyma; a film was left on the surface to allow the skilled execution of the pointed arrises on the Doric columns and the angular fillets on the Ionic. This work was lengthy and expensive and, in the case of some buildings, remained incomplete.

Plates

Paestum – The temples, the 'basilica' and the temple of Argive Hera

59 The so-called 'basilica' dating from the third quarter of the 6th century is the oldest of the temples at Paestum. All that remains are the colonnades of the peristyle (the stylobate measures 179.2 by 80.9 feet with 9 x 18 columns) and part of the inner colonnade. The Doric columns have a strong bulge or entasis which imparts strength to the shafts crowned by wide, loaf-shaped capitals.

60 Detail of a capital. The necking is decorated with downward falling leaves and the base of the echinus is outlined with a garland of lotus flowers arranged in palmettes and rosettes.

61 General view showing the east façade and the long north side of the temple. This gives an impression of the way in which the colonnade unfolds and of the plastic quality resulting from the bulging shafts and the play of light on the fluting. The modeling of the capitals also assumes an important part.

62 Interior of the colonnade.

63 The façades of the three temples at Paestum: in the foreground the 'basilica,' the temple of Athene in the background, and the projecting mass of the temple of Hera in the center.

64 The long south side of the temple of Hera (5th
/65 century) seen through the north colonnade of the 'basilica.' The rather heavy balance of the classic colonnade contrasts with the rough vigor of the archaic style. In the foreground, two capitals from the 'basilica.'

66 Hexastyle façade of the temple of Hera also known as the temple of Poseidon (80.2 by 197.8 feet with 6 x 14 columns). This façade has a strong geometrical rhythm: all its elements (three rough-cast steps, columns, architrave, frieze with triglyphs and unadorned pediment) are composed in accordance with the rules of chill classical porportion.

67 Detail of a capital. The superb classical echinus has annulets in place of archaic decoration.

68 Interior of the peristyle showing the two-storeyed arrangement of the inner Doric colonnade.

69 The long south side of the temple of Hera. The vibration of the light stresses the brilliant harmony of the horizontal and vertical lines.

70 Interior of the cella with the double colonnade dividing it into three aisles. The two-storeyed Doric colonnade is somewhat compressed: it appears very elegant when seen vertically, but, in fact, restricts the interior space.

Aegina – Temple of Aphaia

71 Façade of the temple of Aphaia (the stylobate measures 45.5 by 95 feet with 6 x 12 columns). Note the simple, soaring rhythm of the columns and the harmony of their capitals, almost classical in style.

72 Detail of a capital. The pitted tufa was originally door of the cella.
73 The elegant Doric outer colonnade.

74 Detail of a corner of the outer colonnade. Note the construction of the architrave composed of two coupled blocks.

75 Detail of a capital. The pitted tufa was originally covered with stucco.

Agrigento – Temple of Concord

76 Detail of the Doric order on the exterior.

77 Main façade of the temple of Concord dating from about 430, one of the latest of the series of temples at Agrigento (the stylobate measures 55.8 by 130 feet with 6 x 13 columns). This façade has a complex rhythm. There is a progressive reduction of the bays (10.6 feet, 10.2 feet, and 10 feet) to balance the contractions of the Doric frieze at the corners: on the longer sides the reduction extends from 10.6 feet (width of a normal bay) to 10.2 and 10 feet.

78 The temple of Concord gives the impression of springing from, and forming part of the supporting rock.

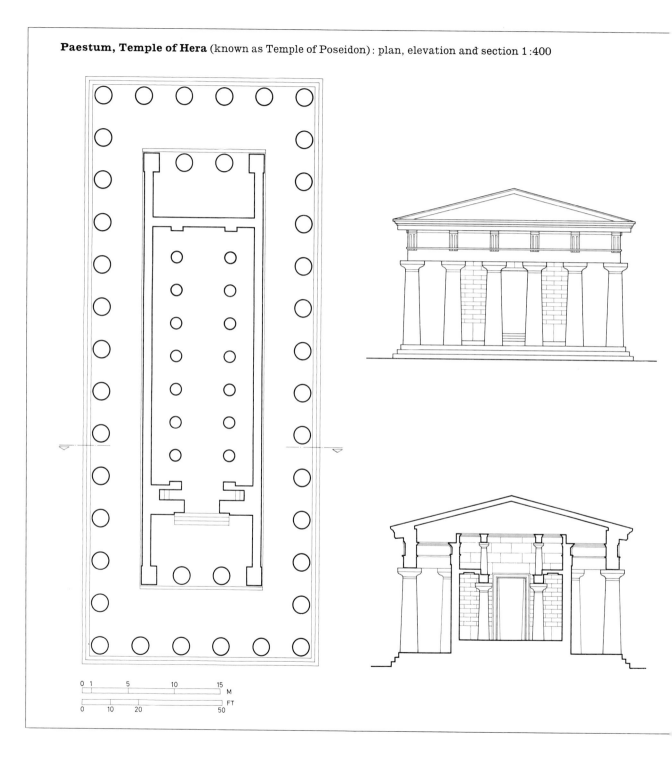

Paestum, Temple of Hera (known as Temple of Poseidon): plan, elevation and section 1:400

0 1   5   10   15
M
0   10   20   50
FT

Aegina, Temple of Aphaia: plan showing position 1:600

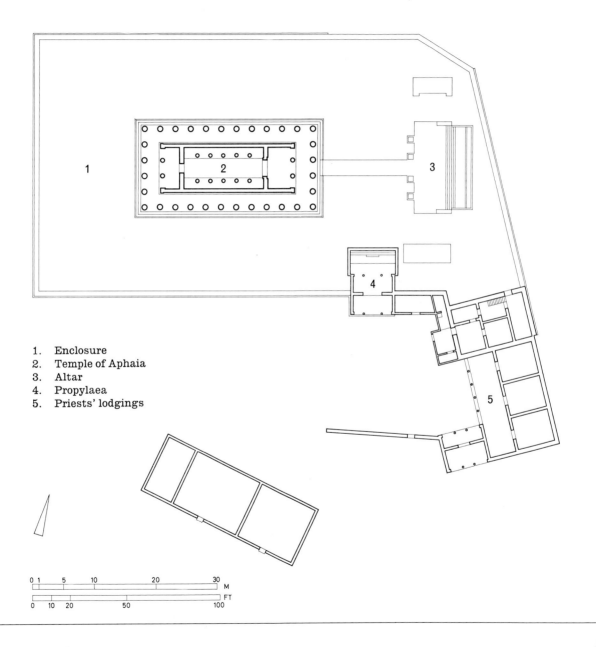

1. Enclosure
2. Temple of Aphaia
3. Altar
4. Propylaea
5. Priests' lodgings

Notes

The Greek temple

It is impossible to discover a prototype for the construction or individual features of a Greek temple in any other building, either within or beyond the borders of Greece. It was produced by a process of evolution peculiar to Greek architecture which, in rapid stages, aimed to endow the dwelling place of the god, the primitive chapel destined to house his image, with a balanced design which could both possess its own unity and be integrated with the other features necessary to the form of worship, such as an altar for sacrifices, esplanades for processions and colonnades for the reception of the worshipers. It should not be considered in isolation but as one, and probably the most important, feature of the whole ensemble of which it forms an integral part. From this standpoint the originality of the Greek temple and its respect for balance and proportion may be all the better appreciated. The isolated chapels of the geometrical period were probably too much like human habitation and too humble and small-scale for a time when sculptors were starting to put into practice the technique necessary for the carving of large devotional statues. At Samos and Corfu we may see the first tentative attempts to envelop the 'naos' with a girdle of columns. The full monumental effect of this device may be appreciated in the basilica at Paestum, even though the cella has disappeared, and in the unfinished temple at Segesta. Many types of solution were adopted to suit individual regions and local tendencies, but the principle of investigation and evolution of plans followed a parallel course.

Paestum

The famous group of temples at Paestum, which are in a wonderful state of preservation, illustrate the amazingly difficult balance which Greek architects had to achieve between the independence of a building and its relationship with its neighbors, between its individual monumental effect and its connection with its landscape setting. Here, in this flat countryside, the temples are set on the main axis of the town, but they have been raised up on slight hillocks which emphasize them and cause them to stand out. The main thoroughfare helped to keep them clear of the bustle of the town without isolating them. Each has an idividual style and independent proportions, and there is an interplay between their massive outlines. Instead of cancelling one another out, they set each other off. The classic balance between the archaic elegance of the basilica and the heavy outline of the temple of Poseidon is achieved by a connection that is hinted at rather than explained. The more distant temple of Athene is decorated in the Ionic style which is powerfully integrated with the Doric buildings and expresses the continual attempts of the regional architects to discover original solutions.

Aegina

The temple of Aphaia at Aegina was built at the turn of the 6th and 5th centuries and belongs to a group which included the temple of Apollo built by the Alcmaeonids at Delphi and the temple of Athene built by the Peisistratids on the Acropolis at Athens. These temples were similar in proportions, plan, and style of decoration and succeeded in elaborating and embodying the discoveries of the archaic period before they became petrified in classical molds. Their aesthetic partly eludes us as their building materials, either tufa or pitted limestone, required a stucco facing with vigorous polychrome decoration that brought the architectural design to life. Capitals were partly painted red, triglyphs and metopes alternately blue and red; moldings and drip-stones were also emphasized by painted decoration. All this made an arresting effect which it was necessary to judge against the luminous sky beneath which the building was set.

The temples of Sicily

Sicily was the chosen land of the Doric style and still provides us with the most astonishing examples of Greek Doric temples. We may follow the stages of their development from the massive temple at Syracuse constructed of vast monoliths, signed by the architect, to the delicately shaped buildings with rich facings of painted terracotta crowning the Acropolis of Selinunte. Temples C and D at Selinunte illustrate the elongated proportions of the early sanctuaries where the colonnade surrounding a cella which was an independent unit. This aspect of independence survives a Segesta where the colonnade stands on its own, since the walls of the cella were, in fact, never built.

Agrigento, Temple of Concord: plan and section 1:300

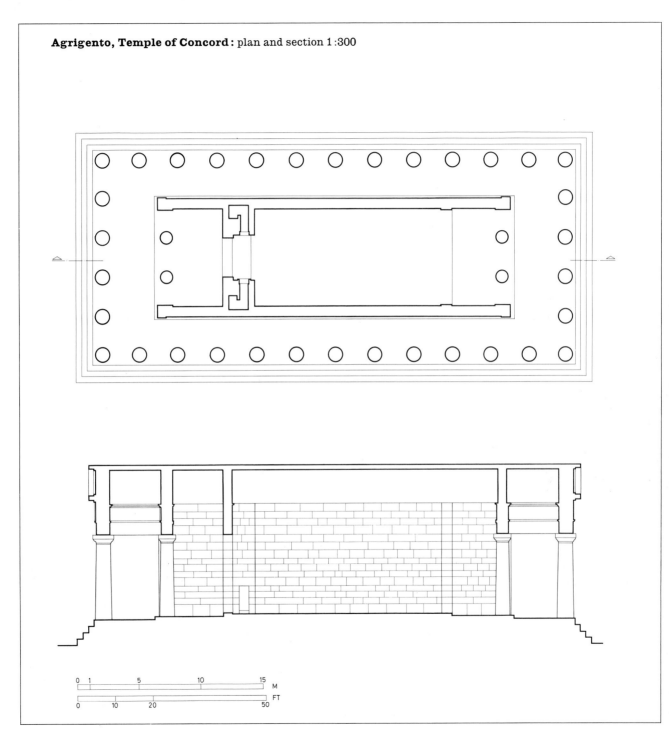

0 1   5   10   15
                                  M
                                  FT
0   10   20   50

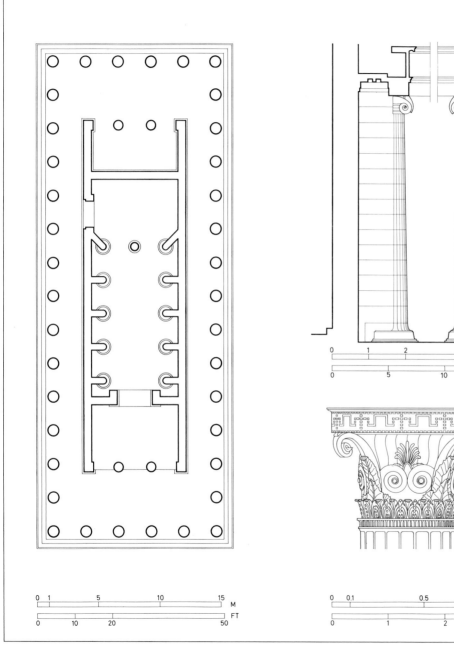

3. Elements and Forms

The part played by isolated supports such as columns and pillars assumes special importance in an architecture making only a very limited use of vaults. There was swift development in this sphere after some groping attempts noted in the early buildings of the geometric period. In the late 7th century the basic principles of portico, peristyle and interior colonnades led to the realization of large scale buildings, and, by the early 6th century, architects were in undisputed control of their medium. The reason for this swift development is still obscure, for it was partly associated with the natural evolution of primitive materials such as wood, brick, and rubble masonry. Forms and motifs were first of all elaborated in these materials and still bore reference to them after their integration in buildings constructed of stone where their functional role ceased to be apparent. Freed from their original purposes, associated with structures where development was denied them and with a material for which they had not been designed, they became molded into rigid types which took a long time to coalesce. Thus, throughout the classic period, the Doric, Ionic and Corinthian styles all kept their individual and sometimes contrasting features.

The Doric style

The Doric order was geographically and traditionally linked with the Dorian and Peloponnesian spheres of influence and was also tentatively adopted in Attica. It is the geometrical expression of the fundamental characteristics of an architecture based on the method of juxtaposition and stacking. By its exclusive use of linear composition it guarantees transition and movement between horizontal planes and vertical features from the base of the stylobate to the top of the pediment. The clear-cut fluting of the columns results in a powerful vertical thrust from the horizontal plane formed by the lines of steps which subtly interrupt the

Reconstruction of the original wooden entablature from which the Doric order derived

sculptured decoration: this took care of the difficult junction between the oblique or rounded lines of the cushion and the vertical surge of the fluting. All 6th century buildings had these fine capitals, each with a wide-spreading echinus whose outline grew steadily thicker as time passed on. Superb examples may be found in the basilica and temple of Demeter at Paestum. The square abacus set on the echinus was the geometrical transposition of the junction between the vertical supports and the horizontal entablature.

Here linear interplay was resumed. With the architrave came a return to the horizontal: it was a completely bare feature, its upper edge bordered by a narrow molding ornamented with guttae, stone likenesses of the bolts used in the construction of earlier wooden entablatures. The frieze was composed of alternating triglyphs with vertical bars and plain or sculptured metopes whose length usually exceeded their height. There has been much discussion regarding the

ascending movement. The irresistible upward surge expressed by the Doric shaft with its twenty channeled flutings finally expands into the capital; it is as if the fluting is halted and consolidated by the necking grooves which form the transition between the shaft and the crown of the echinus, the emphasis of which varies according to period. The motif is stressed and renewed by the grooves accentuating the base of the echinus. These features derive from the origins of the Doric capital whose prototype may probably be found in the thick wedge of the Mycenaean capital. Portrayals of architecture on painted vases of the archaic period show that these capitals consisted of a thick crown separated by a narrow neck from a wooden shaft the upper edge of which was strengthened by a tie. The neck was ornamented with metal moldings which, in the capitals at Corfu and the 'basilica' at Paestum, were transposed into

Development of the outline of a Doric capital

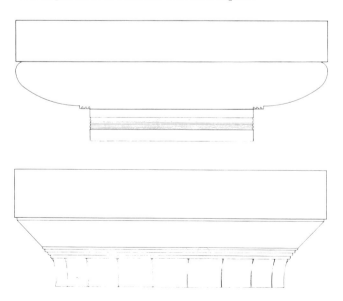

Doric construction: temple of Aphaia at Aegina

set side by side to form a link between the beam of the architrave and the sections of the roof. The bars of early triglyphs must undoubtedly have fulfilled the function of supports; for they were originally always associated with columns and, later, with a building's points of support. Metopes, on the other hand, played a protective part or were used to ensure regularity. It is important to realize that they were the first features of a Doric entablature to receive decoration.

The upper sections were finished off with drip-stones which repeated the horizontal lines of the stylobate and closed the contrasting movement situated between the two planes. Their protective role was indicated by the projections which caused the water from the roof to fall clear of the feet of the columns, and their function was also reflected in their moldings; the upper edges were bounded by hawk's beak moldings which broke up the raindrops and prevented the water from spreading back on to the roof. The soffit was formed of a series of small plaques kept in position with cylindrical pegs. These had played a practical part in wooden constructions but were simply ornamental in larger stone buildings. This artificial arrangement was coupled with strict rulings regarding the rhythm of the frieze in relation to the columns: these imposed contradictory demands at the corners of the colonnade where the triglyph had to be above the axis of the column and simultaneously to form the angle of the entablature. The resulting difficulties, especially the contraction of the spacing at each corner of the peristyle, led to the decline of the order in the early 3rd century.

Doric architecture is essentially linear and geometrical and could only be fully realized in the luminous Greek landscape. The only permissible decorative effect was the stressing of areas of light by bands of shadow at various levels. In the case of the stylobate the lower edges of the

origin of the elements of the Doric frieze. In any case, the origins of the typical classical frieze should be sought in primitive constructional forms of wood and brick with the aid of fictional representations. There seems little doubt that a metope was originally a wood or terracotta plaque closing a gap between piers of brick or wood, or between supports possibly

Ionic capital

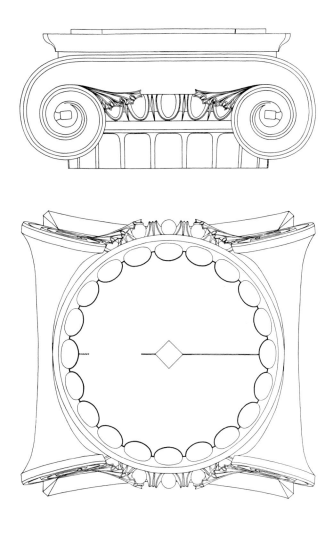

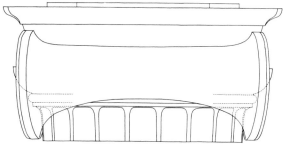

steps were deepened by the use of a plain or double molding; the fluting of the shafts took on bolder relief and an identical part was played by the vertical grooves of the triglyphs in the frieze. In the Hellenistic period the geometrical shape of the abacus was softened by a smooth molding on its upper edge. The soffit of the architrave, the string-course on its forward face, and the articulated soffit of the dripstone were also ornamented with plain moldings. The final touch was polychrome decoration which will be discussed later.

The Ionic style

The Ionic style derived from Eastern lands. Its history is more complex, but, in some respects, more obvious than that of the Doric order. Columns and entablature belonged to an artistic sphere sensitive to the vital part played by decoration and linked plain architectural construction with decorative elements borrowed from the other fields. These included the palmettes, volutes, lotus flowers and egg-and-dart moldings which appeared on furniture, vases, woodwork, sarcophagi and funerary stelae, and metal or terracotta objects. Here, the decoration was not merely functional; it played its own individual part and was applied to all forms.

The shafts of Ionic columns were slimmer, more deeply fluted, and contained between a molded base and a sculptured capital. In its native Asia Minor and in the islands, the order kept a base made up of several superimposed registers with projecting torus moldings alternating with the concave outlines of scotia and hollow moldings. Classical tradition adopted the Attic base composed of a plain scotia between two torus moldings which could be ornamented with plait-work or interlacings as at the Erechtheum or, later, with scalloped leaves. The capital above had its own share of the volutes and palmettes associated with structural ele-

84

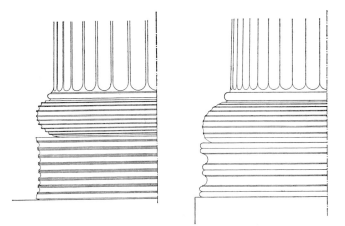

Two types of base for Ionic columns

ments. Originating from a wood pillar holding up a beam by means of a horizontal crosspiece and two slanting buttresses, the Ionic order at first hesitated to stress either of these features by decorating the intermediary sections with palmettes and volutes. The function of the two slanting elements is emphasized in the so-called Aeolic capital from Neandria, by large vertical volutes which curve outwards leaving a gap in the middle which is filled by a vigorous, extended palmette. These volutes are placed above a crown of leaves which marks the transition to the pillar.

Aeolic capital with volutes from Larissa and Neandria

The other type, exemplified by the archaic capitals from Delos, emphasizes the horizontal crosspiece, the ends of which curve downwards and inwards in accordance with the rhythm of large volutes; the crown of leaves is here replaced by a cushion decorated with egg-and-dart. Palmettes conceal the gap left between the crown and the horizontal volutes.

Decorative invention did not end here. The lowest-drums of the columns of the Artemisium at Ephesus were lined with sculptures and, at the Erechtheum, a circlet of palmettes and lotus flowers decorated the upper sections of the shafts. The origins of these buildings were linked with the practical needs of primitive structures. The supports of these ancient buildings may have been in the form of palm trunks or bundles of reeds in eastern architecture, or of stripped tree trunks in the west, but, in each case, they required a facing at both ends, and particularly at the base, to protect them from collapse and damage caused by humidity. This was the origin of the protective panels of terracotta or metal which were ornamented with painted decoration and later with sculptures, when these supports were executed in stone.

Classical taste delayed this extension of decoration which expanded on a lavish scale in the Hellenistic period. Sometimes the entire shaft was covered with an abundance of vegetation; and facings of bronze, gold and silver added to the rich decoration of Ionic and Corinthian columns. The same characteristics distinguished the Ionic entablature. The soffit of the architrave was decorated with plait-work or a molding with scalloped leaves and the architrave itself appeared from the front as three smooth, superimposed courses crowned with egg-and-dart moldings. A sculptured frieze was not an essential feature of the entablature; this was only introduced gradually and with many

Corinthian capital

struck by the sight of a basket enveloped in acanthus leaves set as an offering on a tomb in a necropolis at Corinth. It is of interest to know that this invention was due to a sculptor. The graceful harmony of the acanthus leaf could not fail to attract the attention of Greek sculptors at a time when they sought to animate the rather severe lines of their buildings. Bunches of acanthus were already frequently portrayed on funerary stelae in the 5th century, as can be seen from vase paintings. Of equal significance is the fact that Corinthian capitals began to appear at a time when architects were pre-occupied with the arrangement of interior spaces. The Corinthian order which was slimmer and more decorative than the Ionic and more adaptable to half-columns and pillars, best answered these requirements. The use made of this vegetable order by the architect and sculptor, Scopas, in the temple of Athena at Tegea is a good example of the part it was to play.

For the base and entablature the Corinthian order took over the features of the Ionic almost unchanged. In Greek architecture, however, it long remained a secondary order used to lend rhythm to interior walls or as a constructional feature of small monuments. It was not until the Hellenistic period ended that the order took its place in great architectural schemes.

Roofing

Vaulting played only a minor part in Greek architecture and was never used to cover vast spaces. It was restricted to underground buildings such as tombs or crypts where the earth itself formed a buttress. A few examples may also be found in fortifications, and theater galleries, for the most part in Asia Minor. The earliest examples are in the form of corbeled vaults, possibly imitative of Mycenaean buildings. Skilled Greek stone-cutters also

regional variations. On the other hand, drip-stones with denticles were in regular use; they derived from flat roofs where the ends of the rafters were visible. The whole feature was sur-mounted by a gutter decorated either with human faces or vegetable motifs. This was originally in terracotta but was later built in stone like the rest of the building.

The Corinthian style

The steady intrusion of decorative motifs favored the development of the Corinthian order at the expense of the Ionic. The story of the discovery of the Corinthian capital may not be true but, as so often with the Greeks, stresses the importance of the invention: apparently the first Corinthian capital was executed by the Athenian sculptor and goldsmith, Callimachus, one of the rivals of Phidias, after he had been attempted arched vaults and examples of these may be found dating from the early 4th century in tombs, sally ports and narrow passages. Monumental vaulted gateways forming features of architectural complexes as at Olympia, the agora at Thasos, and Priene did not make an appearance, however, until the end of the Hellenistic period. In place of a vault Greek builders sometimes formed roofs with large inclined slabs supported on their ends and forming an acute angle.

Use of these forms, already known in ancient times, received a fresh impulse from Alexandria and Syria at the start of the 3rd century. The same principle was also employed in Greek buildings of the classic periods when double sloping roofs appeared in some temples including

Vaulting system for a tomb at Pergamon

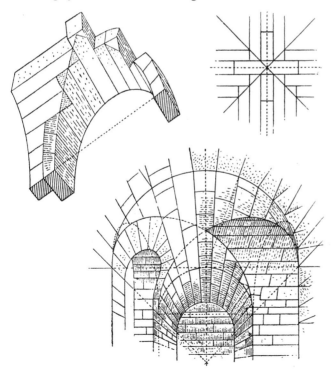

those at Bassae and Stratus in Acarnania. The transposition into stone slabs was not difficult.

The use of semi-circular vaults was at first restricted to funerary buildings such as the Necromanteion at Mesopotamon. There are also frequent examples in Macedonian tombs of the 4th century. The expanded taste for vaulted buildings in the 3rd and 2nd centuries was possibly due to the architects of Pergamon.

Large hypostyle halls and huge two-aisled porticoes were never roofed with vaults. The necessary timber constructions were carried by isolated supports – columns or pillars. Quadrangular and polygonal pillars formed of large blocks were found alongside slim columns. The buildings were usually plain without any special form of decoration, and capitals were simplified Doric. Columns were sometimes replaced by pillars in storeyed porticoes.

Orders with columns or pilasters set side by side against a wall surface were not generally used before the Hellenistic period. Not till then was their decorative value fully realized. The capitals were usually Ionic or Corinthian. Their success was linked with the architects' efforts to lay out interior spaces. The classical temple plan clearly reveals the hindrance imposed by the twofold interior colonnades which divided the cella into three narrow aisles preventing the harmonious display of the statue of the cult. The conquest of interior space resulted from a successful arrangement devized by the sculptor-architect Scopas in the temple of Athena at Tegea in the mid-fourth century.

Special attention should be paid to the corner pillars or antae used to form the end of walls. This arrangement was strictly associated with the peri-style colonnade and the ends of the cella walls. Various formulae were experimented with to resolve the opposition between the shrouded forms of the colonnade and the sharp angles of the walls. In temple D at Selinunte, at Paestum and the treasury of Cyrene at Delphi, the walls were terminated by half-columns which formed a transition with the columns. This device did not earn wide acceptance as it was regarded as a solution lacking architectural clarity. In other cases a pillar was set against the wall end but not integrated with it: this formula was adopted in all the archaic buildings at Paestum. The architects of the classic period preferred to express the supporting function of the end of the wall which upheld the frieze of the vestibule, usually with the help of two or more columns 'in antis,' by reinforcing its thickness and applying a corner capital, though the anta itself was not separated from the wall. The blocks of the anta were in fact hewn to resemble a pillar, but the rhythm of courses and joints was not broken. The style of the capitals was regulated in accordance with the order chosen for the colonnade. Doric capitals were distinguished by their severity; their plain moldings were sometimes heightened by painted motifs and they were crowned with pointed hooks. The Ionic capitals of Asia Minor were decorated with superimposed rows of egg-and-dart and palmettes projecting over one another. Those used in Attic buildings, on the other hand, were less elaborate and had a simple egg-and-dart decoration.

Ceilings, roofs and timberwork

The employment of columns and isolated supports involved the general use of timber framework for roofs and combinations of wood and stone for ceilings.

The ordinary type of ceiling made of planks resting on joists calls for no particular comment. Important constructions, such as temples and public buildings, were enriched with coffered ceilings. The supporting beams rested on

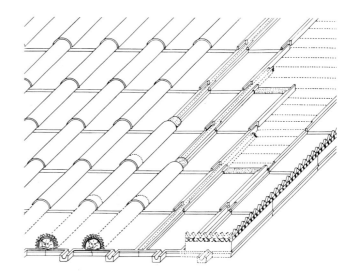

Roof with flat tiles and cylindrical junction plates

the masonry of the portico, the top course of which was set with a smooth abacus. The upper faces of the beams were trimmed in accordance with a procedure still followed by stone-cutters and carpenters. Coffers and caissons ringed with wood fillets were then set on this assembled framework.

This type of construction connected with woodwork and carpentry techniques was, nevertheless, translated into stone and, as a rule, temple peristyles were covered with coffered ceilings .hewn in this material. The soffits continued to be ornamented, the ridges and backgrounds of the coffers being given over to floral motifs, usually roses, convolvulus or lotus flowers.

The absence of vaulting sometimes proved an obstacle to architects obliged to construct interior spaces suited to the housing of tall statues and large-scale offerings. A special type of ceiling was often used in such cases: one with a double slope, consisting of two inclined planes resting on a ridge pole. This arrangement resulted in a twofold slope rising to a point. Thanks to this device the temple of the seven statues at Delos and the temple of Apollo at Bassae were able to accommodate the effigies of the gods on their lofty pedestals.

Moreover, a taste for simple buildings prevented the general development of ceilings. The Greeks were perfectly satisfied with fine timberwork supporting roofs of terracotta or marble. No trace of ceilings has been found in the great stoas of the classic and Hellenistic periods or in the great hypostyle halls like the one at Delos.

Greek architects, as distinct from those of the East and the Aegean, never adopted the use of flat roofs after possibly experimenting with them in some archaic buildings. Even the little votive aedicules of the geometric period, hewn and molded after the fashion of full-scale buildings, were given roofs with twin slopes. The remains of the temple of Prinias in Crete and the form of some terracotta friezes discovered in Asia Minor, however, presuppose the existence of flat roofs, probably made of beaten earth. The climatic condition of the Greek mainland, on the other hand, led to the general use of sloping roofs along with terracotta or marble tiles. The habitual use of tiles is attributed to the Corinthians, of marble to the islanders of Naxos. There is also some documentary and archeological evidence pointing to the additional employment of metal. The extremely high price of metal, however, prevented this from becoming general practice.

Standard forms of tile which scarcely changed until the end of antiquity came into being in the late 7th century. Two main types used simultaneously. The predominantly rectilinear Corinthian style employed wide, flat tiles with rims at the sides and junction plates triangular or polygonal in outline. The Laconian tiles, on

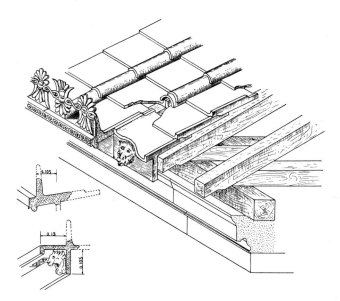

Canopied molding with anthemion

the other hand, were all curvilinear and, size apart, were almost identical with the round tiles now used in Mediterranean countries. Both types, whether executed in baked terracotta or hewn in marble, were on a large scale: the usual length was about 1.6 feet but this could rise to about 3 feet. They matched exact models which were officially executed for public works.

Gutters and rainwater spouts

From the archaic period onwards, roof edges were accorded special attention for both practical and religious reasons. The edges of flat roofs in the East and the sleeper beams which supported the timber roofs of western buildings were both vulnerable to bad weather. For this reason terracotta features in the form of friezes or coffering were set on the upper levels of buildings, and the edges of twin sloping roofs were heightened to form gutters pierced with rainwater spouts. There were experiments with various forms in the archaic period before the traditional type of guttering was evolved. This was shaped like an ogee and was surmounted by tile ends fitted to the end piece of each row of junction plates. They had openings through which the water could flow out; originally provided with terracotta conduits, they were later treated as waterspouts with lion heads.

The surfaces of these terracotta plaques were decorated. In Ionia, friezes depicted processions of animals and human beings. Similarly, there were representations of gorgons or of gods denoting divine protection. In the west figurative representations were restricted to the tile ends. The coffers and gutters were accorded a more geometrical painted decoration of meanders and stylized water-leaves alternated with palmettes and lotus flowers.

Section of roof with a layer of clay beneath the tiles

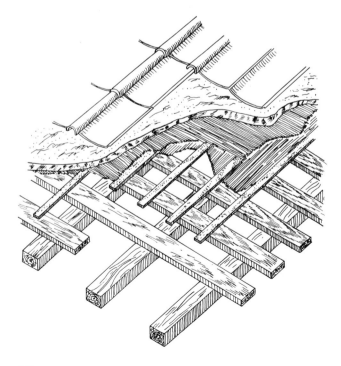

Timber framing

The outer roof was supported on a system of timber framework. A few archaic buildings such as the treasury of the sanctuary of Hera at the mouth of the Sele, and some 4th century tholoi, prove that Greek builders were able to construct quite complex frames with the timbers radiating from a center truss. These required skilled adjustment, but the more usual principle was extremely simple. This was based on the traditional framework consisting of a ridge-beam and rafters finished off by purlins. In the stoas the ridge-beam was very often abolished and the rafters rested on a ridge-tile supported by the middle colonnade. The richly forested regions of Macedonia, north-west Asia Minor, the Peloponnese and southern Italy provided the necessary materials and the timber trade was directed with great exactitude. The commonest woods were pine and fir; oak was already seldom used. Costly woods such as cypress from Egypt were reserved for exceptional buildings like the Parthenon.

Tiles were laid either directly on the rafters or else on a more compact series of battens. Apparently only the border tiles were fixed with metal pegs which were meant to steady the entire roof covering. To avoid the danger of a subsidence the tiles were sometimes set on a bed of clay or reeds, probably recalling the construction of primitive roofs. This layer of clay, though mentioned in several texts, was not as widely used as has sometimes been maintained. The Greeks did not hesitate to mix materials in order to lighten their roofs. There is evidence that some temple roofs had border tiles of Parian marble but the rest of terracotta. Some buildings were also partly roofed with sheets of copper or bronze – a rare luxury.

Lighting

The relatively simple plans used by Greek

architects did not result in the tricky lighting problems presented by the complex, monumental buildings of the Egyptians. Nevertheless, various and frequently ingenious solutions were devized.

In the first place, the number of temples generally supposed to have been roofless has been shown incorrect. Temple G at Selinunte, however, remains an exception and the temple of Apollo at Didyma consisted of a richly decorated enclosure surrounding a space for the oracle. On the other hand, the tholoi at Delphi and Epidaurus, the temple at Bassae and all the great temples of Sicily and Asia had roofs.

Most of these temples have surprising absence of light openings, apart from the main door. Often, indeed, light penetrated only through the great entrance arch, which was already shadowed by the peristyle colonnade. It must be borne in mind, however, that the temple was only the dwelling-place of the statue of the god, where the public did not enter, and that sacrifices and the laying of offerings took place at the altar outside. A peculiar solution was adopted in the Parthenon and at Olympia to break the area of shadow and bring the chryselephantine statues of the divinities to life: a sheet of water was placed between the door and the statue so that the reflection of light from the door shed spotlighted the gold and ivory statue. Roofs were lit by 'opes,' tiles with a circular opening, the edges of which were raised to prevent the passage of rainwater.

More instances than is generally supposed occurred of windows placed on either side of the main door to increase the light inside. There are traces of these in one of the temples on Delos and it is possible that this plan was also adopted in the tholos at Epidaurus. The Greeks made windows with transoms and wide bays separated by small columns set in the intervening wall.

The openings were closed by grilles. There is evidence of this arrangement in houses on Delos and in the assembly halls of the Hellenistic period at Priene and Miletus.

In buildings whose function and interior space demanded a brighter light the Greeks revived the device of the lantern currently used in Egypt. The central section of the roof was raised and the bays in the wall dominating the lower level were left open. Examples of this may be found in the telesterion at Eleusis and the better known hypostyle hall on Delos.

Decoration and polychromy

Form and function were strictly associated in Greek architecture. There was thus no place for decorative features or motifs independent of the structure or superimposed on any of its functional elements as in eastern or Roman architecture. Columns existed as supports, never as decoration applied to arcades or walls which also played a purely architectural role. Decoration could also only be functional.

Throughout the development of the Doric order, moldings remained severe. They were smooth, of linear composition, and sometimes emphasized by painted motifs; their effect was entirely confined to contrasting hollows and reliefs and the interplay of light and shade. Stylobates and the outer faces of entablatures were to a slight extent enlivened by grooves, fillets and string-courses, while the horizontal lines of the upper parts of buildings were stressed by restrained hollow moldings and ogees. It was not until the late 5th century that hollow moldings appeared behind the mutules of dripstones and the facings of gutters were carved with scrolls and volutes borrowed from the Ionic order. Towards the end of the 4th century in Ionia, the bare edges of the abaci of Doric capitals were ornamented with fillets and quarter hollow moldings which were sometimes repeated on the upper edge of the triglyph. In the 3rd century the soffit of the architrave was usually ornamented with a rounded molding flanked by two small hollow moldings.

With the Ionic order moldings were livelier and richer because they were ornamented with sculptured motifs, set at different levels of the building. At the feet of walls and columns, scotia and torus moldings, ornamented with plaits, meanders and interlacings, eased the transition between the stylobate and elevation, while on the entabablature, architrave, frieze and dripstones, were articulated by similar moldings. Courses at the tops of walls were covered with palmettes which were sometimes repeated on the necks of columns echoing the motifs of the capitals; these emphasized the echinus, the abacus and the cushions of the volutes.

The late 5th century saw the introduction and expanded use of the acanthus leaf. This followed the development of the Corinthian order and formed its essential feature, especially on the capital. In the late Hellenistic period, it ended by spreading over the whole entablature. At Alexandria it formed a basket from which the column sprang; later it had to contend with the development of the scroll of ivy or vine leaves which twined round columns and spread over pillars and the smooth surfaces of the frieze. Henceforward decoration tended to mask architectural features.

Moldings cannot be separated from the difficult and controversial problem of polychromy. Traces found on newly excavated architectural features leave no doubt as to the significant use of painting. We must, however, beware of excessive generalization, according to which Greek buildings constituted real polychrome pictures. It has been established that

moldings which are now bare were often ornamented with painted decoration, even in the Doric order. Surfaces were not as denuded as they appear today but were painted in strong colors; reds, blues, ochers and yellows. Whole elements including capitals and all sections of the entablature were probably covered with paint. Traces of painted ornament, especially egg-and-dart and palmettes, have been found on Ionic capitals and corner pillars. Triglyphs and metopes were also touched up with paint; lines and contours were stressed by strong colors but there is no evidence that they were transformed into large painted panels. Plain surfaces were avoided on terracotta facings and metopes, areas where painting was fully justified and where, indeed, it originated. Against a neutral

Arrangement of sculptured decoration at the Parthenon

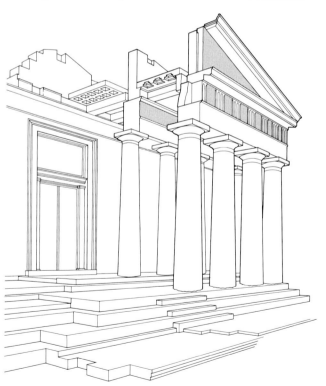

92

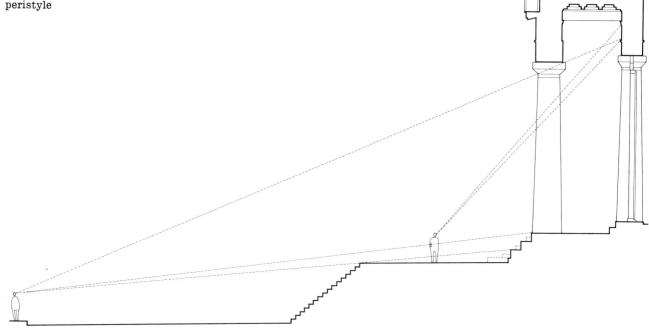

Sight-lines for the continuous frieze set beneath the peristyle

background in which the natural color of the clay was maintained by means of a glaze, the framed decorations included representations of men and animals.

No aesthetic judgment can be passed without some consideration of Greek landscape. In the strong light brightest colors are acceptable and pastel colors seem faded. Even shadows share this luminous quality; thus, many architectural features are set in the shade cast by projecting moldings or superimposed elements of the entablature. Instead of black shadow, there is an even greater luminosity which deadens contrasts and accentuates the sculptured effects continually sought by Greek builders.

The part played by sculpture

The essentially plastic character of every branch of Greek art ensured that their craftsmen came to grips with the problems set by the necessary connections between sculpture and architecture. Moreover, work at the Parthenon was directed by Phidias himself, the greatest sculptor of the classic period, and the conquest of volumes and interior space was basically due to sculptor-architects such as Theodorus and Scopas. Sculptured decoration was introduced and developed in certain sections of buildings where the architectural construction caused empty spaces, especially at the level of the frieze and within the typanum of the pediment.

There were, undoubtedly, other attempts to find solutions. The lower drums of the Ionic columns of the temples of Ephesus in Ionia recall the decorative schemes of the East where sculptured friezes were widely used to ornament stylobates. This link is also preserved in the superimposed friezes of the funerary monuments at Xanthus whether they are in the pure Lycian tradition as on the acropolis, or completely hellenized as in the case of the monument of the Nereids. In the mid-4th century, the Mausoleum of Halicarnassus still had friezes round the stylobate. These sculptured friezes were most commonly used, however, in the upper portions of buildings where they became regular classical features set between the architrave and a course of dentils. They satisfied the Ionian taste for long literary accounts and painted or sculptured renderings of hunts, warlike exploits, races, and religious and mythological subjects. The formula was even employed in Doric architecture; in the Parthenon it was placed within the shadow of the peristyle.

On the exterior, the Doric order favored

Example of decoration of a triangular tympanum: Temple of Artemis, Corfu

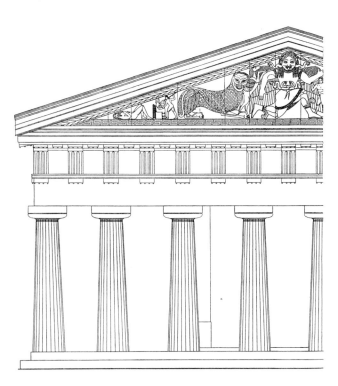

sculptural representations within the restricted frames of the metopes. These imposed limitations which ran counter to Ionian temperaments and did not suit all subjects. This may be seen at Assos where a procession of horsemen was, contrary to custom, carved on the architrave, and at the temple of Hera at Paestum where the movement of the dancers in procession round the frieze is interrupted by the triglyphs.

Finally, the triangular tympana formed by the pediments at each end of the building offered an excellent site for sculptured decoration. Throughout the 6th century it is possible to follow the progress made by sculptors in their attempts to adapt themes and compositional formulae to fit the space inside the pediment. Their preoccupation with religion was primarily expressed by the appearance of the protective gorgon in the center; this motif was flanked by reclining animals. Eventually, complex scenes or whole dramas were portrayed by concentrating the chief characters in the center of the tympanum, while secondary aspects or spectators were set on either side in the angles of the pediment. Technically this led to the gradual detachment of the sculpture from the background of the tympanum. In the 5th century, the characters were executed in relief and moved freely in space.

It must be noted that the material and technical demands attendant on the limitations of framed metopes and pediments only exercized a very slender influence on the choice of themes and subjects. The nature of the divinity, local traditions, and the individual concerns of the cities played decisive parts.

Architecture and mathematics

The geometrical rigidity of Doric architecture and its aesthetic discoveries based on linear relationships and the simple proportions of surfaces and volumes led to the linking of architectural composition with mathematical expression. These works of architecture were certainly laden with mathematical symbolism. Their chosen proportions and the relationship between the dimensions of a building and one of its features such as a column, frieze or doorway must have been dictated by the anxiety to express plastic forms in relation to abstract mathematical formulae. This fascinating hypothesis has been taken as a starting point for the study and interpretation of several buildings. In this sphere it is important to define the value of the results obtained, the extent to which they can be relied on and the direction set by the hypothesis.

There is undeniable evidence that Greek architects and sculptors were preoccupied with these matters. They were sensitive to proportion and sometimes wrote commentaries, which have unfortunately not survived on their buildings. Polycleitus the Argive sculptor, for instance, wrote a treatise on the 'Kanon,' and in the 6th century Chersiphron, and later Ictinus, Pythias and Hermogenes published works on architectural proportion which were summarized by Vitruvius. In their buildings the architects of ancient Greece methodically sought to realize perfect harmony of proportions based on what they called 'summetria,' the 'commodulatio' of the Romans. This meant the internal balance of the parts, the relationship between the parts and the entire composition established on the module, a unity which was apparent throughout the building.

The application of these principles may be directly discovered from a study of the buildings where comparisons may be established between the dimensions of the main features – between the heights of columns and the diameters of their bases, between their diameters and the distances between them, between the height of the entablature and that of the columns. Vitruvius used these calculated variations to distinguish different types of colonnade – eustyle, diastyle, pycnostyle and so on – but they also have a chronological significance for the architectural historian. Bearing in mind the building, its materials, and regional traditions, the grouping of particular connections can provide useful evidence regarding its place in a chronological series.

Furthermore, the determination of the module (the base diameter of an Ionic column, the diameter of the lower or center part of a Doric column) allows us to establish the chief dimensions of a building in whole numbers and to formulate the geometrical squared plans, horizontal and vertical, on which its components are based. This simple, empirical process corresponds to the working methods of the architects of antiquity, at any rate up till the 4th century and later. They often proceeded by the application of old formulae and limited their creative powers to a system of simple connections in which surfaces and spaces were assembled together untroubled by problems involving spans and thrusts which were to arise in more complex forms of architecture employing vaulting.

This search for proportion was by no means limited to the outward forms of buildings. It lay at the center of architectural creation. Applied to lines, surfaces and spaces, proportion is the organizing principle of every architectural creation which is thus transformed into pure mathematics. The best system of proportion is based on what Renaissance artists, reviving antique tradition, called the golden or divine proportion. The determination of the golden section and golden number is merely the algebraical expression of the well-known geometrical theorem of Euclid: to divide a given length into two unequal parts so that the ratio between the shorter and the longer is equal to the ratio between the longer and the given length. This proportion may be expressed geometrically by the construction of a triangle or square and corresponds to an algebraical equation $x^2 - x - 1 = 0$, whose root is $x = \frac{1+\sqrt{5}}{2}$, or the irrational number: 1,618,033 . . . The geometrical expression of this proportion, in the form of a triangle or square, plays a considerable part, both in nature and the arts. In studies on the golden number, this irrational number and the corresponding geometrical figures are symbolized by the letter 'psi.'

In architecture, plans and façades may be transposed by this link into terms of plane geometry and the organization of interior space into volumetric geometry.

The geometrical constructions corresponding to the arithmetical ratios are triangles, squares, and rectangles, the perfect rectangle being the one where the ratio between the sides is equal to psi. These shapes, in addition to their mathematical connections, have an aesthetic significance.

In the same way, spatial geometry allows us to define the corresponding polyhedrons – those drawn by Leonardo da Vinci to illustrate Fra Pacioli's 'Divina proportione' (1509) in accordance with Plato's definitions.

Hence the historian of Greek architecture is faced with the problem of whether it is possible to rediscover the Platonic principles, the golden number and the corresponding shapes in the building, by reducing plan, elevation and interior spaces to geometrical shapes expressing the number psi, the triangle psi, the rectangle psi, or the starred pentagon.

We may, perhaps, go a step further and suppose that 4th and 3rd century architects were sufficiently influenced by Platonic specula-
tions that they sought to transpose some mathematical problems into terms of architecture. Just as the proportions of the door were supposed to represent the irrational number psi, the ratios between the diameters of the columns and the dimensions of the metopes probably illustrated the duplication of the circle, a much discussed problem in the 4th century. Such tempting hypotheses are, however, based on insufficient or uncertain architectural data, but they do have the distinction of stressing the primary part played by masters of geometry and mathemathics in Greek architecture.

In this architecture it was the line alone which counted, and harmonies were simple. The rhythm of the Parthenon colonnade can be defined by proportional numbers identical with those making up the Pythagorean scale. The diameter of the angle columns, the diameter of the ordinary columns, and the intervals between them, correspond to all the intervals and harmonies of the diatonic scale which follows on the celebrated universal proportion of 6, 8, 9, 12, attributed to Pythagoras. This may have been deliberately worked out by Ictinus or, again, just a happy chance. Nevertheless, it is more or less impossible to enclose the plan of the Parthenon in a network of triangles and pentagons, as no line in the building is really straight; they are all connected to counter the optical distortions which affect purely geometrical shapes when exposed to the luminous atmosphere. This is the paradox of an architecture outwardly so geometrical. In fact, it is wholly made up of curves: the curve of the stylobate echoed in the entablature, the entasis of the columns, the inclination of the columns from the vertical both towards the interior of the building and the center of the colonnade, the accentuated effect of the walls enclosing the cella in tapering lines.

Plates

Bassae – Temple of Apollo

101 Temple built of local limestone, set in an arena of mountains. The orientation is unusual, with the main façade facing north.

102 Detail of the outer columns with their vigorously hewn fluting. The ridges react harmoniously to the play of light.

103 Interior of the cella. In the background the sole remaining base of one of the middle columns in the central axis.

104 The interior niches on the west side seen through the wide opening of the main door. Note the grooves for fixing the wooden jambs on the upright.

105 Detail of the base of one of the interior half columns. An unusual outline formed by a high hollow molding set on a splayed base with a smaller hollow molding. The junction with the shaft is marked by a torus.

Segesta – Temple

106 General view of the remarkable landscape setting of this severe, powerful building.

107 The temple of Segesta blends with the landscape emerging from it as a natural feature.

108 Detail of the site. The stylobates formed of coupled slabs have kept the tenons used in the transport of the blocks.

109 Detail of the rough-cast work. Its horizontal lines describe a curve which stresses its function as a support for the vertical line of columns with their clearly defined undulating rhythm.

110 Detail of the corner entablature.

111 Interior of the colonnade showing the inner arrangement of entablature and pediment.

Athens – Temple of Athena Nike on the Acropolis

112 Detail of the Ionic order. The base is composed of a large scotia contained between a reduced lower torus and a thick, fluted upper torus.

113 General view of the temple framed by the Propylaea. Sculpture and architecture emphasize the part played by it as the virtual prow of the Acropolis.

Didyma – Temple of Apollo

114 The gently sloping vaulted corridor leading to the inner court.

115 The inner court with a ramp (50.2 feet) of 24 steps framed by the two doors of the vaulted corridors.

116 Detail of the steps and their retaining walls.

117 Surviving columns on the north outer peristyle. They were 65 feet high, of very slender proportions, and supported an entablature which was very light compared with the proportions of the building. It was 10.9 high, one sixth of the height of the columns.

118 Decoration of the base of the walls of the pronaos and the cella. It consists of a deep scotia contained between two sculptured torus moldings.

119 Base of the standard columns; two molded scotiae set on a square plinth, surmounted by a fluted torus.

120 Decorative motifs of the heads of the capitals (above) and of their sculptured bases (below).

121 Detail of flat and relief chiseling.

Ephyra – Nekromanteion

122 Main hall of the Nekromanteion. Walls of heavy rusticated masonry supporting upper levels in brick.

123 Subsidiary halls. Masonry.

124 Subterranean chamber for consultation of the oracle, with arcaded vaulting.

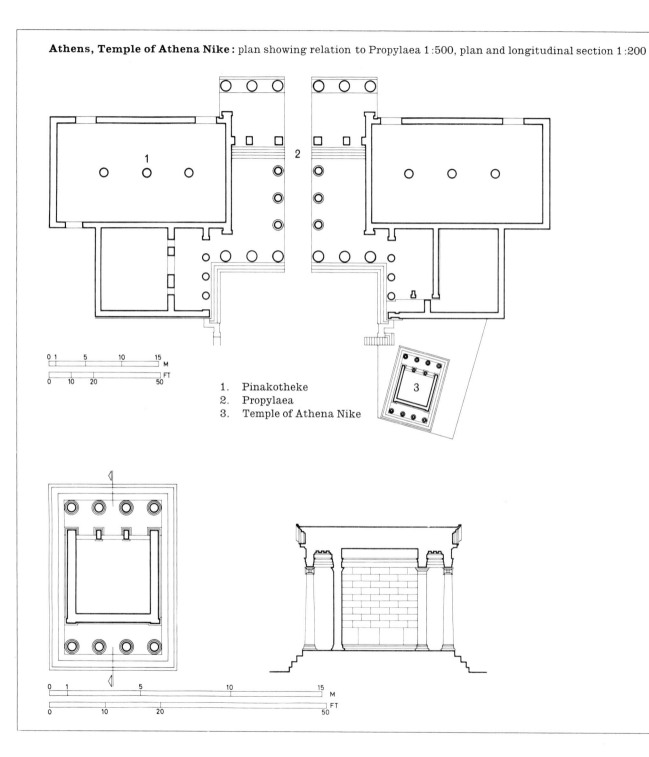

Athens, Temple of Athena Nike : plan showing relation to Propylaea 1 : 500, plan and longitudinal section 1 : 200

1. Pinakotheke
2. Propylaea
3. Temple of Athena Nike

Didyma, Temple of Apollo: plan, elevation and cross sections 1:750

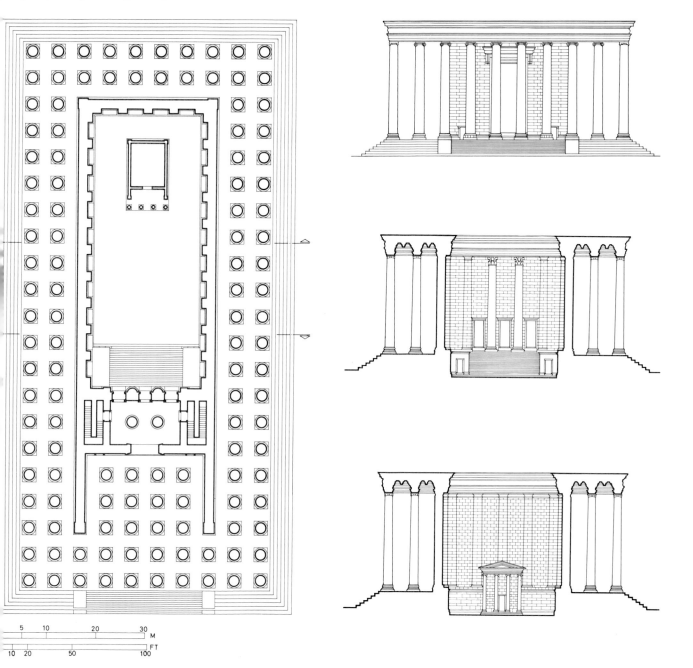

Notes

The Acropolis at Athens and Ictinus

The magnificent building program at the Acropolis occupied less than twenty-five years and it is possible to name many of those who had a share in the work. Pericles must be credited with the inspiration of the creative work and with having procured the means of its realization. Phidias certainly played an active part in the design; he was probably in command and, beyond all doubt, hard to please, imposing his rulings on Ictinus who successfully adapted a difficult program to suit his countless demands, translating it into a conception harmoniously blending fertile invention with strictly observed tradition. He was certainly helped in the execution by Callicrates who was a clever technician, though not an original creative artist, and the work was brought to a splendid conclusion by Mnesicles who was responsible for the Propylaea. It would be a great advantage to have more detailed knowledge of the development of the work and the specific creative periods. In connection with the advance in architectural composition which enabled buildings of such varying and individual characteristics to be grouped together without losing their separate identities, it is unfortunate that we cannot make better sense of the few indications provided in an inscription made by Callias about 435; it is possible that this mentions a plan for the layout of buildings on the Acropolis. This must have been a turning point in the history of architectural creation when the personality of the architect became more consciously subservient to the requirements of a master plan. Collaboration between artists, respect for the exigencies of ritual and regard for vested interests provided a harsh school for the Athenian architects working on the Acropolis site. The formulae adopted in the individual cases of the Parthenon, the Propylaea and the Erechtheum reveal the complexity of the set programs. It is not surprising that the plans and types of buildings remained in isolation, since each was inspired by the individual exigencies of its site.

The temple at Bassae

The temple at Bassae stands at a height of 3600 feet in the heart of the mountains of Arcadia which here lie open towards Ithome and the west coast of the Peloponnese. It has the feeling of local work although Ictinus may have contributed to the design. He certainly knew how to rediscover the original inspiration of his native land if it is indeed true that he was the pupil of Libon who built the temple of Zeus at Olympia at the beginning of the century. We may recognise his characteristics and his readiness to invent original formulae in this conception of an interior plan dispensing with the traditional three narrow aisles constricted between two-storeyed colonnades still in use in the Parthenon. It was left to Scopas many years later to make a definitive adjustment of interior space, but Bassae had already opened the way.

Didyma and the Ionic order in Asia

To understand the plan and scale of Didyma we must first recall its function as an oracular center. As at Delphi and Clarus, the oracle of Apollo was associated with a spring found in the inner court; when a Byzantine basilica was set above the ruins of the temple, this spring was respected and again included in the building. The water gushed from the depths of a cleft in the layers of limestone forming the plateau of Didyma and was the heart of the sanctuary, the adyton; it was enclosed in the holy precinct of the temple and a small chapel close to it housed the image of the cult. This adyton was enveloped in a massive architectural composition consisting of the exterior wall forming the boundary of the court and the double colonnade of the peristyle. The foot of the peristyle steps, set on the rock, was 11.6 feet above the interior level. Access to the adyton was by means of two vaulted corridors opening into the huge pronaos which was treated as a hypostyle hall of twelve columns. The traditional monumentality of Ionian architecture with its increased scale due to the joint influence of Egypt and the East found full expression in the extravagant colonnade where the bases of the columns forming the façade were decorated with sculptured panels. The temple at Didyma reveals the Ionian taste for great architectural massee adapted to the needs of the primitive elements of ths oracle. The dipteral plan of the peristyle and the dimensions of the pronaos resemble those of the temples at Ephesus, Samos and Sardeis. The classic taste of Pythius may have curtailed the part played by sculptured decoration in the temple of Athene at Priene, but the architects of Didyma certainly rediscovered the Ionian love of magnificence. The bases of the center columns of the façade added sculptured panels mingling plant motifs and spirited figures to the established outline.

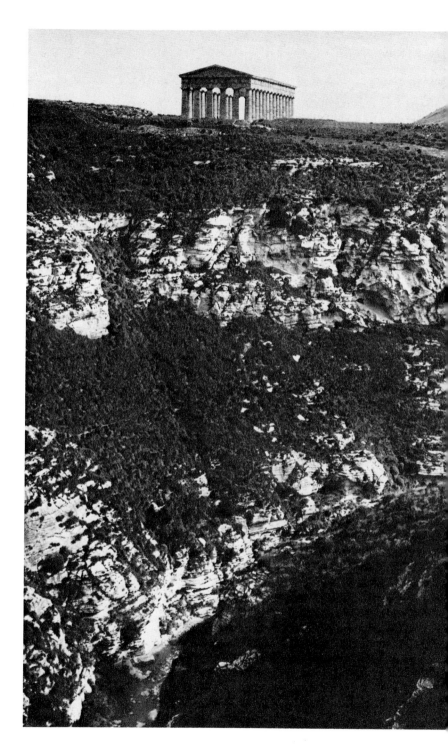

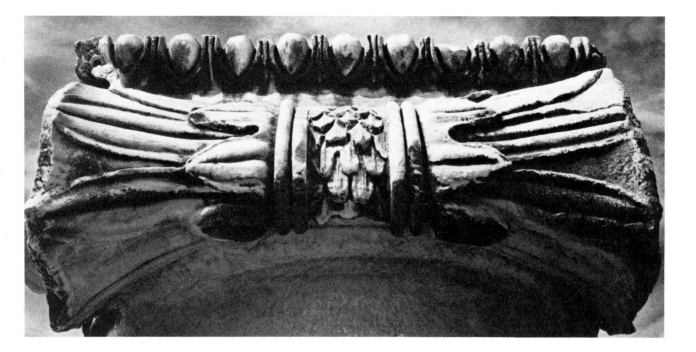

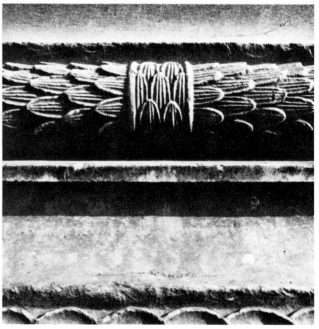

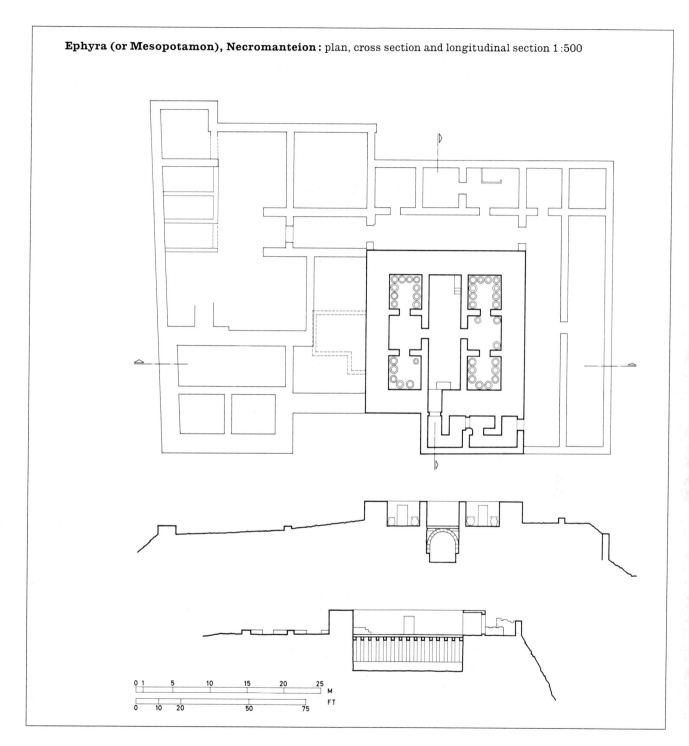

Ephyra (or Mesopotamon), Necromanteion: plan, cross section and longitudinal section 1:500

Priene, Bouleuterion: plan, longitudinal section, elevation and cross section 1 :300

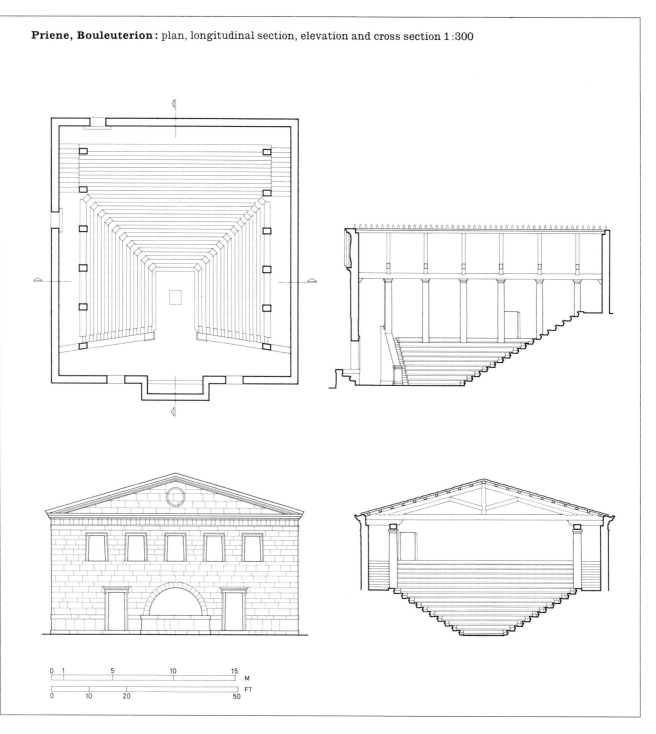

4. Important Stages of Architectural Creativity in Ancient Greece

Discoveries of the archaic period: the invention of the colonnade and the conquest of masses

The primitive aspects of Greek architecture cannot be summarily defined. So many different experiments and formulae were tried out before the emergence of the structures of the classic period. Greek architects subdued their materials to the needs of their technique and conceptions before creating their final forms and styles.

They swiftly assimilated a plan which caused Greek temples to be derived from the Mycenaean 'megaron.' This, in turn, had been developed, to suit the needs of the palace, from an older, more widely used plan which had already appeared at Troy in the early part of the second millennium and was connected with various aspects of continental Helladic civilization. The palaces of Mycenae had been reduced to such utter ruin that a revival of their style in Greek architecture was on a highly restricted scale, apart, perhaps, from the use of this rectangular hall of continental origin which, with its hearth, formed the nodal point of the palace. In the islands, and in Crete, other forms existed and attempts were made to revive them. There was no feature of this early architecture, however, which could have served as a model for the peristyle plan which enclosed the rectangular cella in a continuous colonnade where space and light blended with the mass of the building in accordance with a conception purely Greek in spirit. This inspiration did not reach the Greeks by way of Mycenaean or Aegean architecture. Even in those cases where there is possibly some Egyptian influence, the buildings have been hellenized and their colossal scale has been reduced to a human level.

The conquest of plans and forms by the Greeks occurred in two stages. No large project was realized before 600, because available materials were not suited to the early conceptions of the second half of the 7th century. As long as limestone and marble were not used, Hellenic genius could not find an outlet for its expression. Thus, from 800 to the end of the 7th century, innumerable experiments were all based on a light form of construction employing wood, clay and marble. Then, at the turn of the 6th century and with the final conquest of materials, there was a creative surge of forms and styles. In less than a hundred years all buildings were constructed in accordance with rules and standards which only had to be exploited in the classic period to result in the creation of masterpieces of balanced harmony.

a. First attempts at an architecture of wood and brick

The first traces of Greek architecture of the period ranging from the late 9th to the mid-seventh century are small, but none the less diversified. The Greeks recovered slowly from the Dorian invasion and the Achaean migrations, and, starting with traditional ideas and new beliefs brought by the invaders, or from the East, created fresh conceptions and forms of gods more in keeping with the developing social and political order; they could, however, find no remembered pattern for temples or religious buildings. Indeed, the first type of house they provided for the gods was little different from those of mortal men. Using inherited constructional procedures — rubble and clay on a stone pedestal consolidated by wood frames and bonds — they built small rectangular or apsidal temples of which the Heraea at Argos and Perachora are examples. In every holy place on the Greek mainland, there are remains of these early, horseshoe-shaped temples; their façades had a small flat-roofed porch supported by two columns and backed by a two-sloped roof.

Experiments all over the Greek world included

the excavation of complex, half-ruined Minoan palaces for the purpose of providing new buildings. Temple A at Prinias was rectangular in plan with an opening on the narrow side, but the uneven rhythm of the façade with a square pillar on the axis of the pronaos seems to have been derived from Minoan vestibules. The same rhythm recurred in the interior where two columns on the central axis of the cella framed a rectangular altar. This type of temple was widely found up till the 6th century in the islands and the Aegean coastal regions.

Halls of oblong plan were also in the Minoan tradition; their main façades, with one or two columns dominating the entrance, were on the longer sides of the buildings. To this type belong the temples at Gortyn and some of those on Delos and Samos. The first example of adding

Terracotta model of the Argive Heraeum

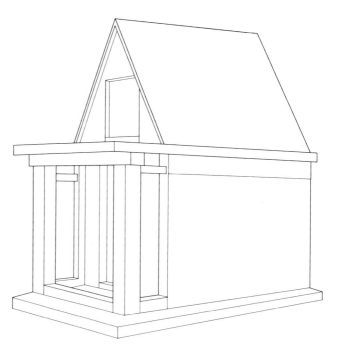

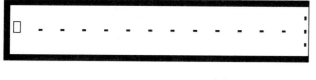

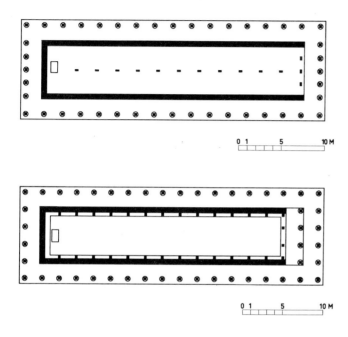

Three stages of the development of the Hecatompedon at Samos

long or, more precisely, 100 Samian feet; hence its name, the first Hecatompedon. The rough brick walls were set on a base of rubble, and the hall, whose eastern end was open to the sacrificial altar, was divided into two aisles by a row of center supports – wooden pillars resting on stone pedestals. The statue of the goddess, the base of which has been unearthed, was situated at the back of the hall hidden by the line of pillars. This was still a clumsy conception with the architectural composition in the geometrical style like the sculpture of the period. The relationship between masses and volumes was still only felt in two dimensions. At the turn of the 8th and 7th centuries, the temple was radically transformed for practical, religious and aesthetic reasons. A gallery was constructed right round the early cella to protect the rough brick walls from the rain. The proportions of the building remained unchanged but the dimensions were now 121.8 feet long by 30.7 feet wide. For the first time the house of a god was accorded a monumental character. A rhythm was introduced into the composition between a hall with solid walls and a colonnade whose seven façade pillars balanced the features of the cella. This uneven number resulted from the relationship of the center pillar to the central row of interior supports and of the outer pillars to the ends of the walls.

This provided a vital impetus. Less than fifty years later a new temple was built after the older one had been destroyed and the rhythm of encircling colonnades formed part both of the sanctuary itself and of the neighboring buildings. The exterior colonnade was on a larger scale and had added width on the façade owing to an intermediary row of columns placed between the end of the walls and the outer edge. This heralded the dipteral plans so much favored in Ionian countries in later centuries. The colonnade gained individual significance. The side gallery was widened and, inside the

to the monumental nature of a building by the addition of an exterior gallery to the rectangular cella is at the Temple of Hera on Samos. In its successive development, from about the year 800 to the late 6th century, it provides highly typical examples of progressive experiments with monumental masses offset by colonnades, though these have only wooden pillars.

About 800 B.C., the humble temple was replaced by a hall of peculiar construction. Though only 21.5 feet wide, it was 108.6 feet building, the central row of supports was abolished, creating a free space more suitable to the display of the statue of the goddess. The pillars were set back against the walls. This was a new solution, probably in advance of its time, as several centuries were to pass before the constructional demands were resolved by comparable formulae which resulted in the development of interior colonnades; these were, in fact, too restrictive, but became an established feature of the classic period. South of the temple, a double aisled portico 231 feet long formed a monumental setting to the consecrated esplanade containing the temple and the altar. In this way, the Samian architects of the mid-7th century conceived the earliest realization of an ordered architectural composition based on a plastic conquest of space. The materials were still, however, brick, rubble and wood.

b. The architects of Iona and the Ionian style

The creative spirit exemplified in the second Temple of Hera at Samos emerged in the early 6th century in several individuals described in contemporary accounts and whose work can still be seen in remains at Samos and Ephesus.

For the first time, architects' names can be associated with large-scale schemes. Theodorus of Samos who was both engineer, architect, and sculptor seems to have worked both for Rhoecus in Samos and Chersiphron and his son Metagenes at Ephesus. Pliny the Elder and Vitruvius refer to Theodorus and his treatise, written in conjunction with Rhoecus, on the Ionic temple which they both helped to build. They were both theorists and practising architects; they had an active interest in all kinds of experiment, and also visited Egypt. In addition, the rich and prosperous cities of the coast of Asia Minor and the adjoining islands rivaled one another in their attempts to gain the services of the best artists. All this points to the favorable conditions allowing this early school of Ionian architects to achieve some of the most splendid examples of Greek architecture.

Theodorus and Rhoecus may have taken the idea for their vast colonnaded layouts, which the Greeks came to call labyrinths, from the Egyptians. None the less, the germ of the composition already lay in the second Hecatompedon built in the mid-seventh century. Added scale and harmony, an improved relationship between the various parts of the building, closer connection between walls and supports, and a subtle relationship between the divisions of interior and exterior spaces all helped to transform a crude building into a noble ensemble.

This Temple of Hera was 346.5 feet long and 173.3 feet wide with an exterior colonnade of 104 lofty columns. These rested on a wide platform slightly raised above the ground which had been leveled and drained by Theodorus in his capacity of engineer. The cella had a vestibule open to the exterior and was divided into three aisles by a double row of 15 columns. The walls were made of local limestone, the columns of the outer colonnade, of marble, their rhythms adapted to the interior divisions; on the façade open to the east, were eight columns corresponding to the two rows of the peristyle, the ends of the two walls of the cella and the two inner lines. The bays were irregularly spaced, varying from 28.4 feet in the center, to 20.2 feet at the corners. The rear façade of 9 or 10 columns echoed the rhythms of the side bays.

Rhoecus had scarcely finished the building before it was destroyed by fire and replaced by a similar construction commissioned by Polycrates, tyrant of Samos, who employed Eupalinus of Megara. Meanwhile, Theodorus was summoned to Ephesus where he collaborated with Chersiphron in building the great Temple of

Artemis. Both proportions and plan were identical with those of the temple at Samos. Remains, together with the rebuilding of the temple after a fire in the 4th century, have resulted in more accurate knowledge of its detail. Not every city was able to produce so imposing a building and its proportions exceeded those normally found in Greece. They were seldom imitated except in a few cities with unusual resources such as Sardeis, the capital of Lydia, and the wealthy Sicilian colonies of Selinunte and Agrigento.

Such endeavors have not made the task of defining the Ionian style any easier. Even at the outset there were two contradictory types of capital. Both were derived from pieces of timber used to relieve the weight of an architrave on a wood pillar and were two different attempts to resolve the placing of the decorative volutes; it is impossible to say which stemmed from the other. The capitals at Ephesus decidedly direct the style towards a horizontal arrangement of the volutes which were first painted or carved on a piece of wood placed horizontally between the cushion surmounting the column and the beams of the architrave. The so-called Aeolic capital, on the other hand, developed the volutes vertically; they were placed as decoration on two oblique pieces of wood which parted at the top of the pillar to widen the carrying surface. The vertical section, or intervening space, was ornamented with a wide palmette. This motif of the twin, vertical volute was known in Assyrian and Phoenician decoration of the 10th and 9th centuries and probably made its first appearance in archaic architecture. Its development was limited geographically to the coast of Asia Minor north of Smyrna and the island of Mytilene.

c. The Doric style and the conquest of the masses

In the East the Ionian architects developed buildings on a large scale, revealing a skilful aptitude for composition which, though complex, retained its lightness and freedom of decorative expression. On the Greek mainland and further west, however, the Doric style developed more geometrically and with stricter rules.

These experiments were more or less contemporaneous; for the building of the first stone Doric temples at Delphi, Olympia, Corfu and Syracuse also began about the year 600. As in the East, the first peristyles were built of wood in accordance with a utilitarian design: this has been proved by the successive arrangements discovered around the site of the Temple of Apollo at Thermum. Features of the columns of the first Temple of Athena Pronaia at Delphi also show that the proportions of these colonnades could be relatively slender and airy. Yet very soon the main features of the Doric style were recognized as solidity, the purely linear, geometrical relationship of the individual features and the firmly established balance of the assembled masses. The substitution of stone for the lighter and more supple wood and brick probably increased the builders' difficulties, and resulted in proportions becoming heavier; but, on the other hand, this did not apply to the Ionic style.

A building like the Temple of Apollo at Syracuse, one of the earliest Doric attempts at a peripteral plan, bears witness to the clumsiness of the first Doric architects of the western world. Its proportions are lumpy, both in plan and elevation, and the oddity of the stone cutting is apparent even in the foundation where the last two steps are hewn from a single block. The outer colonnade is exceptionally thick, an effect not lessened by the irregularity of the bays (12.5 feet on the façade and 11 feet along the sides) and the diameters of the columns (6.6 feet along the façade and 6.1 feet along the sides). There are six columns along the façade and seventeen along the sides, all monoliths, 23.8 feet high. Their close grouping and sharp tapering help to abolish the rhythm of gaps and solids usual in peristyle colonnades.

If we follow the development of the temples of Selinunte in accordance with the traditional chronology, we may well believe that their successive states accorded with those of the temples of Samos. The first buildings seem to have been narrow, elongated cellae consisting of a single hall divided by two or three interior columns into two aisles and a more or less square adyton. Although the megaron of the sanctuary of Demeter was probably roofed, the buildings of the Acropolis were possibly no more than consecrated enclosures, wholly or partly open to the sky. There is no proof, as at Samos, that these halls were later enclosed by peristyles, as none of the cellae in the 6th century temples, C, D and F has an inner colonnade. Elsewhere, the link between cella and peristyle colonnade remains vague and uncertain; they have an independent rhythm, except in the Temple of Apollo at Thermum where the portico of the peristyle enclosed a pre-existing cella.

In all these early Doric buildings, spatial arrangement and the connections between the different masses were much less cleverly carried out. From the beginning the Doric order was characterized by an obvious lack of skill.

Nevertheless, a firm balance was attained in the Temple of Apollo at Corinth, dating from the second half of the 6th century. Here the relationship between length (177.5 feet) and width (71 feet) is distinguished by six columns on the ends and fifteen on the sides, an almost classical ratio. The cella, with pronaos and opisthodomos 'in antis' is divided into two halls, the first rectangular, divided into three aisles by two rows of four columns, the second almost square with a ceiling supported by four columns. The relation-ship between the supports of the cella and the peristyle columns is already regulated by classic laws, in accordance with a subtle interplay based on tangents instead of axes as in the great temples of Samos and Ephesus. In this case archaic architecture attains full strength.

d. Interchanges between the two styles

The rich invention enlivening the end of the archaic period in the second half of the 6th century, the travels of artists, and colonial migrations necessarily brought about interchanges in the Greek world.

It is known that the Dorian and Attic regions borrowed from the repertory of Ionic architecture. At Athens, the Peisistratids wished to rival the Ionian tyrants by building a great temple dedicated to Zeus. The early forms for this building were undoubtedly Doric, but the conception of the plan, the general look of the temple and the arrangement of masses were derived from the impressive temples at Samos and Ephesus. It even included a 'forest' of columns aligned in accordance with a dipteral plan in a double colonnade on the long sides and in three rows on the façades. The dimensions, 135.6 feet by 355.7 feet, make the builders' intentions clear.

At Amyclae in Sparta, in the heart of Dorian territory, the Lacedaemonians commissioned Bethycles of Magnesia, an Ionian architect, to design the strange throne of Apollo. He combined a Doric order with motifs introduced from his native land. Ionic consoles and moldings and widespread volutes enlivened the severe look of the monument.

In the West the roughness of the colonial Dorian style was softened through the medium of settlers from cities employing the Ionic style.

A splendid capital discovered near the Vieux Port at Marseilles shows that the Massiliots erected an impressive Ionic temple in the late 6th century. Rich decoration extended to many features, particularly the rings ornamenting the upper sections of the shafts.

Similar, though less bold, inspiration lent a touch of originality to the buildings of Paestum towards the late 6th century. The general arrangement was probably based on Doric conceptions, but the plan of the 'basilica' with its central colonnade, its placing of nine columns on the façade, the wide space of the gallery surrounding the cella, and the structure of walls and antae reveal a spatial and rhythmic conception more Ionic than Doric. The Temple of Athena, sometimes known as the Temple of Ceres, serves as the most noteworthy example of efforts which were made, towards the end of the 6th century, to modify Doric buildings by the introduction of Ionic features. In the first place, it is the earliest example of a mixture of orders which was not to become the rule for another century. A prostyle plan was adapted for the cella as at Selinunte but, after the fashion of the Ionian architects, this was stressed by the choice of the Ionic style for the row of interior columns. The exterior entablature, above the colonnade of the peristyle, was enlivened by an unusual course, above the triglyph, introducing an egg-and-dart pattern. Finally, the dripstone did not have the usual shelves ornamented with drops; instead, the soffit was decorated with painted coffers whose surfaces were enlarged by the exceptional spread of the eaves.

Combination of Doric and Ionic orders in the temple of Athena at Paestum

Conversely, there was a strange intrusion of the Doric order in the last quarter of the 6th century at Assos in the Troad. An elegant temple in the Doric style was erected on the Acropolis but, owing to its proximity to the great achievements of the Ionian architects, it fell under their influence. At first glance the plan appears to be pure Doric, but there are no antae at the ends of the cella walls, as in Ionic temples. The distribution of the columns and their slender proportions also denote local influence and differ from the customary arrangements observed in Greece and the West at the same period. Moreover, there is evidence of a strange adaptation of the Ionian taste for a sculptured frieze to suit a purely Doric structure. A continuous frieze, representing a procession of horsemen and centaurs, is carved on the architrave which is then surmounted by the traditional Doric frieze of triglyphs and metopes. The metopes very likely had further sculptured decoration. Contrary to the custom of the West, the pediments were left bare. This was the general rule for the Ionic temples of Asia Minor.

These experiments, realized both in the East and in the West during the vigorous but rather disordered expansion of this period of archaic art, had no immediate continuations. The rules for each style crystalized at the end of the century, and only later came the evolution of composite forms, condemned as decadent taste.

e. In search of plastic architecture: the Treasuries

The small building known as 'thesauroi,' or treasuries, which played an important part in the embellishment of Hellenic sanctuaries, originated both from the piety and rivalries of the Greek city states. They were offered to the gods as tokens of gratitude. Outward indications of power and often ostentatious, they nevertheless are of high significance in architectural history. Very often they are in a better state of preservation than larger buildings. They also reveal the ancient Greeks attitude to architecture: buildings were also works of sculpture so that the two arts were often associated in the search for plasticity.

These buildings were of restricted proportions – the Treasury of Siphnos at Delphi was 20.2 feet by 28.4 feet and the Treasury of the Athenians 22.1 feet by 31.7 feet – but were carefully balanced and elegantly constructed; there were also numerous variations of design both in the Doric and Ionic styles. They were frequently conceived as supports for rich decoration. At Olympia the treasuries were grouped on a terrace bordered by a stepped ramp, and their richness was emphasized by their splendid terracotta facings. The most magnificent was probably the Treasury of Gela whose superstructure was fashioned to receive plaques of

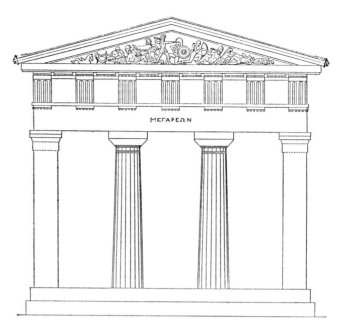

Façade of the treasury of Megara

brilliantly painted terracotta. Huge discs covered with geometrical motifs set in concentric circles enlarged the normal lines of the pediments and hid their upper angles; in this way traditional formal designs were radically modified.

At Delphi, sculptures were linked with all the architectural lines and frequently transformed them. The rich façade of the Treasury of Siphnos was loaded with sculptured forms. Columns were replaced by two caryatids with tall baskets decorated with reliefs on their heads; at the base of the walls and on the entablature courses carved with egg-and-dart, palmettes and heavily modeled lotus flowers formed architectural panels in relief. Sculptures abounded on a continuous frieze encircling the building and also spread over the pediment contrary to the traditional ruling of the Ionic order. The many fragments of caryatids preserved in the museum at Delphi show that the Treasury of Siphnos, which the city built about 525 with the wealth acquired from its gold mines, was preceded and followed by similar buildings. The foundations of buildings of this type sprang up all along the Sacred Way from the sanctuary entrance to the open space before the Temple of Apollo. The taste for sculpture led to further variants including the façade of the Massalian Treasury in the sanctuary of Athena below the famous Castalian spring.

The development of city states and the creations of civil architecture

Early attempts to create architecture were primarily devoted to religious building and the basic temple form was undoubtedly established during the archaic period. Nevertheless, the attempts by the tyrants in the second half of the 6th century to plan and embellish their cities should not be disregarded. Polycrates of Samos, the Cypselids at Corinth, and Peisistratus and his sons at Athens commissioned contemporary architects and engineers to establish large-scale water supplies and greatly increase the number of fountains on the public squares and at road junctions. These became such well known features of everyday life that they were frequently depicted on black figure vases. With the expansion of the social and political frameworks of the city states came the creation of an architectural setting designed to suit the life of the community. This became the symbol of the states' independence and autonomy and molded the real faces of the towns.

a. Expansion of forms and styles of the archaic period

The impetus accorded to religious architecture in the 6th century continued without any major change. It is important to note that creative efforts during this period were clearly restricted to the Greek mainland. The Ionian cities, after their conquest and destruction by Persian armies and administrators followed by Athenian oppression, had neither the means nor the freedom to sustain their creative efforts; for a time they fell back to rebuild their ruins. There was no sign of a revival on the eastern shores of the Aegean until the 4th century. On the other hand, resources were available in the West and there was great building activity at Selinunte, Agrigento, Syracuse and Segesta. This, however, tamely followed the example set by previous generations, adopting the classic laws originating on the Greek mainland. There was a reduction of the elongated proportions of the archaic period and façades were normally built with a prostyle pronaos clearly differentiated from the closed rear wall of the adyton. The last

Temple of the Olympian Zeus at Agrigento, with Atlas figures between the engaged Doric columns

temples at Selinunte and Agrigento were given an opisthodomos and a pronaos with two columns 'in antis,' like those in Greece itself. Local or archaic peculiarities disappeared. The one original program to make an exception to this general rule was at the Temple of Olympian Zeus at Agrigento. With its length of 363.3 feet and width of 173.9 feet, it exceeded the proportions of all other known Doric temples and had certain features in common with large-scale Ionian designs such as the height of the stylobate which acted as a podium and the uneven rhythm of the pillars of the façade. The interior and exterior arrangements were quite distinctive, however. The plan included a false peristyle, the Doric columns were engaged in the walls and transformed into rectangular pilasters on the interior side. They had no drums, but were embedded in the masonry, continuing the courses of the walls. In each bay, the figure of an Atlas set on a plinth halfway up the wall, supported the architrave on raised arms. These figures blended with the courses in the same way as the columns. On each façade, seven engaged columns continued the rhythm of the walls matching those of the larger sides. Entrances were formed by two open doors at the corners; these led into the two side aisles bounded by pilasters engaged in the partition walls. According to Diodorus, the temple was never completed and remained unroofed.

In Greece itself, building continued in the late 6th century in accordance with the same conceptions. The Temple of Athena on the Acropolis at Athens, the Temples of Apollo at Delphi and of Zeus at Olympia, and the temple at Aegina all had the same features with slight variations: a Doric peristyle surrounding a cella divided into three aisles by two rows of interior columns arranged in two storeys. The best example still to be found of this traditional design is at Paestum. The temple at Aegina, after its recent restoration, also clearly evokes the construction of these buildings with its markedly well balanced exterior. The interior, however, is rather confined and too obstructed by the two-tiered columns.

It needed the intervention and collaboration of the sculptor, Phidias, and the architect, Ictinus, to break this tradition with the Parthenon. Their achievement here was to attain a complicated balance for the proportions of the order while breaking new ground with their innovations. The conception and drawing up of the plan were undoubtedly due to Phidias whose aim was to assemble a frame best suited to display the effigy of the goddess. This explains the enlargement of the interior space, the reduction of the width of the galleries to increase the area of the cella, the reduction of the pronaos, and the adoption of eight columns for the façade. The interior colonnade kept the division into two storeys but no longer bounded a narrow central gallery. It took on added breadth and formed a frame for the statue. The archaic arrangement of two halls survived, however, but here again there was a noteworthy innovation: the rear, square hall, the 'Maiden's Chamber,' was given four Ionic columns whose slender shafts rose straight to the ceiling without an intervening storey. This provided a solution to the obstruction of interior spaces of which later architects were to make good use.

An examination of the plan reveals Phidias' conception of the division of interior spaces; these were developed at the expense of the volumetric connections between peristyle, gallery and cella, formerly considered essential. In the actual execution, however, a series of experiments and barely calculable corrections stressed the lines and proportions of the order. Into an architecture which made its effect by the interplay of straight lines and the association of plain, rectilinear masses, Ictinus introduced at all points optical corrections to bend and curve the straight lines. On the horizontal level, the base was outlined by a curve from the lowest course of the foundations up to the stylobate. This curve was echoed as far as the entablature. All the vertical lines were inclined to give the whole composition a pyramidal construction. To reduce the swollen effect of the entasis, the shafts of the columns were given a double inclination towards the axis of the colonnade and towards the interior of the building. This movement of the outer colonnade was clearly perceptible from within the galleries, so that the cella walls forming its background could not be set vertically. Thus the cella, too, was modified by a twofold movement. The walls were inclined, like the columns, towards the interior of the building and were also subservient to the entasis which corrected the angle of the incline. In this way walls and columns were carried in a single sweep and, by means of this subtle interplay of optical correction, the various features making up the building were linked in an individual harmony. It was a dangerous game for anyone without the skilled sensitivity and collaboration of sculptor and architect to play.

b. The architecture of city states

Proud of their autonomy and independence, the city states were careful to defend it and also to give visible proof of it in buildings whose significance was often symbolic. This resulted, in the 6th and, even more so, in the 5th century, in the opening up of a new field of military, civil and state architecture. In this territory the Greeks produced a few buildings which were to remain the keypoints of the antique world.

Ramparts and town walls

According to Aristotle, ramparts were both a means of defence for a city and a decorative aspect of its wealth and personality. Plato, on the other hand, who was also a political theorist, was not in favor of them.

It has been confirmed that, if an acropolis had ancient fortifications sometimes connected with a Mycenaean fortress, then the town walls are relatively recent; moreover, it is difficult to find examples previous to the late 6th century. Cities surrounded themselves with walls through need of military defence and independence.

Just as the fortress on the acropolis had symbolized royal or aristocratic power, so the great town wall was the mark of an independent political community. For this reason the extent of the wall was often out of proportion to the site of the city. It was primarily a defence organism and was outlined so as to make the best use of the surrounding terrain. The extent of the wall built at Messene by Epaminondas in the 4th century and of the wall at Megalopolis was, in each case, almost 6 miles. This length was due to the need to construct a vast stronghold for troops rather than fortify a city whose built-up area only occupied a few acres. In this way, both the town and its surrounding region were protected.

The ramparts were built to a simple design. The rhythmic deployment of their curtain walls followed the contours of the ground; they avoided a geometrical plan and were independent of the layout of the town and its houses. Indeed, the theorist advized that a road should be left between the rampart and the houses to allow the rapid circulation of troops. Excavations have shown that this was so, except when, as at Olynthus, the houses formed the actual rampart.

The curtain walls were interrupted by circular or rectangular towers. At first they were placed at the weakest points, on corners and flanking gates, but in the 4th century, their number was increased so as to reduce the length of wall within range of missile weapons. The rampart was surmounted by a wall walk bordered on the outer edge by a rhythmic succession of coping stones whose outlines enlivened the landscape of ridges and small depressions overlooking the city. The towers included several rooms and were one or two storeys higher than the wall walk. Their walls were pierced by loopholes allowing the discharge of defensive weapons. In the archaic period the towers were also surmounted by an open terrace edged with battlements, but, later, these were covered. With the development of siege engines, especially stone throwers, surer protection had to be devized for the defenders of the rampart, and the wall walk was given a roof. At the same time, platforms were set up for the installation of defensive engines used to hurl projectiles on to the heads of the besiegers and to destroy their machines.

The beauty of these ramparts lies in their perfect adaptation to its function, their use of materials and their constructional technique. Indeed some were masterpieces which rank with more lavish and famous buildings.

Originally ramparts were more often built of brick than stone. Rough bricks dried in the sun offered excellent resistance to the blows of a battering-ram, and this type of rampart was used until the Hellenistic period.

Not every city could provide marble ramparts like those of Thasos, Priene, or Samos. Here they tried to enhance their brilliance by inserting darker courses of gneiss, resembling the timber bonds in brick walls. Materials for ramparts were quarried locally: fine limestones were used in the Peloponnese, Phocis and Boeotia; at Sicyon on the shores of the Gulf of Corinth, beds of tufa provided the long, regularly cut blocks for the town wall, while the towns of Acharnania had walls of dark limestone blending with the tones of the landscape. This identical coloring of terrain and city was particularly noticeable when the same materials were used for ramparts and buildings: granite at Samothrace, yellowish clay at Alinda, volcanic andesite at Assos.

The wall's defensive role and its aesthetic significance were expressed in its constructional technique and in the style of the masonry. The general tendency was to outline the strength and roughness of the material. Archaic walls built of polygonal blocks with hammered facings were best suited to illustrate these primitive characteristics. Later, when more finished trapezoidal masonry and regular masonry with courses of identical height replaced the curving arabesques of the primitive haphazard joints, an identical effect was produced by the refinements of hewing and setting. However the blocks were shaped, the joints were hollowed with a beveling tool which outlined the courses with patches of shadow cast on the sun-bathed surface of the curtain walls. In addition the facings were given prominent bulges; these were sometimes hammered out, sometimes worked with a pointed chisel and carefully rounded so that they stood out even more distinctly from the chamfered joints. Some of the retaining walls of the theater at Dodona, at Miletus and Priene illustrate these systematic investigations carried out by architects of the classic period.

The agora and civil architecture

This is connected with a fundamental law of the Greeks' architectural aesthetic — the adaptation of technique and cutting to suit the material and the relationship between constructional methods and the functions of buildings.

Towards the end of the 6th century, the political communities of the city states began to create the monumental backgrounds suited to the various aspects of their activities. Temples and sanctuaries had originally formed the centers of political life, but they no longer answered the states' full range of functions. Cities needed places of assembly, meeting halls, administrative and business centers. These buildings corresponded to the political, commercial, educational and artistic activities of the city.

The creation and development of civil architecture in the Greek cities was centred on the agora. Originally this was no more than a fairly regular square set around the primitive temples and altars of the divinities of the polis which assumed the protection of the town and its inhabitants. On these esplanades, later to become architectural entities linked with the development of Hellenistic town-planning, there rose groups of original buildings.

The agora was the setting for the development of the Hellenic stoa. These were simple in principle and constituted a basic feature of the architecture of public squares where they played a twofold part. Their galleries and rooms which often served to double the width of the colonnade housed magistrates' offices, merchants' shops, and commercial warehouses. This was the part played by the great Hellenistic porticoes including the Stoa of Attalus at Athens, the great stoas at Miletus, and those of later trading cities. They had their individual functions and were treated as separate entities architecturally. These elongated, seemingly monotonous buildings, with their long rows of uniform colonnades were brought to life by an astonishing interplay of light and shade.

It is the application of this principle that justifies their second function as compositional features. In the late 7th century, the Samian architects erected a long portico with wooden pillars near the second Hecatompedon in order to trace the first outline of the sacred square where worshipers and religious processions were to circle the altars. The systematic use of stoas in sanctuaries and on public squares did not develop until the 5th century. The colonnaded portico became a feature imparting regularity, forming a boundary to an open space and, at the same time, establishing a link between the buildings scattered round it; it formed a backcloth against which the shapes of the main buildings were silhouetted. When the stoas did not fulfil a practical function, they were easily changed into exhibition galleries.

Assembly halls

The earliest administrative buildings, especially assembly halls, were extremely modest in appearance. Originally, as can be seen from many passages in Homer, meetings of chiefs and popular assemblies took place in the open air under the divine protection of an altar set on a paved area in front of the prince's dwelling. In later years popular assemblies continued to sit in the open air in meeting places of which the Pnyx at Athens is a good example. This consisted of a huge platform where the people were massed behind the wood benches reserved for the magistrates and orators; hewn in the rock beside the altar of Zeus where the preliminary sacrifices of purification were offered, was the tribune where the great orators delivered their stirring speeches. Soon, however, the more restrained meetings of the councillors and the activities of the supreme magistrates came to require different buildings.

The Bouleuterion, or council hall, was arranged in accordance with a strictly functional plan. The first buildings designed for this purpose, like those in mid-fifth century Athens, were rectangular and had benches for the senators on either side of a center gangway after the fashion of the British House of Commons; the traditional semicircle was

139

abandoned. Gradually this was changed to a square plan with three sides occupied by tiered seats and the fourth forming an entrance. In the center space was an altar dedicated to the god of assemblies or the divinity of the polis. The best preserved and most evocative example of this type of building in the Bouleuterion at Priene. Its proportions are restricted and perfectly suited to the scale of this small town which constitutes a more or less ideal image of a Greek city. Its south side had an opening below the great sacred portico forming the north side of the Agora. On the other three sides were set the tiers of seats, hewn from local marble. Pillars on the diagonals of the square supported a timber roof which did not impede the vision of the assembly. The outstanding feature of the building is its bareness, symbolizing the overall preoccupation with politics current in Greek city states. The simple beauty of this building was not lacking in grandeur; the quality of the finely hewn, unfaced material, the firm lines of the interior, and the significance of the visible timber roof. Later, the same conception was applied to more imposing halls at Assos and Miletus.

The prytaneum, or seat of a city's supreme magistrates, was rather more complex although just as plain in style. These officials were members of a college, took their meals together and, during their limited period of office, watched over the continued development and maintenance of the state. One of the halls was set apart for the cult of Hestia, the hearth, in which the protecting deities of light and political tradition could take part. Finally, the standard weights and measures, archives, and diplomatic documents, were kept there in one or more storerooms. The building was usually rectangular in plan with various groupings adopted for the different rooms. At Athens, the Prytaneum in the 6th century took the form of a building of several rooms set round a trapezoidal court with a colonnade, but, about 470, this was changed into a circular plan and formed the tholos of the Agora. The neighboring building of the Metroum housed the archives.

The late 5th century Prytaneum at Delos was a fine example of a municipal building of this type with the various architectural features required by its several functions linked to a well defined, balanced plan. This consisted of a rectangle with the longer sides running from north to south. The main south façade had an entrance portico of four Doric columns contained between two lightly projecting bastions. This resembled a theater proscenium or a propylon whose central section is set between two massive constructions as in the design of Mnesicles at Athens. It is uncertain whether or not there was a storeyed colonnade with a loggia. The bays of the central colonnade led to a vestibule extending the whole width of the building; a marble bench ran round the foot of the walls. Beyond this vestibule lay a paved courtyard. The northern section of the building was perfectly symmetrical. A central north-south partition formed two rooms to east and west, each preceded by a vestibule. The eastern vestibule contained two columns between pilasters which gave the succeeding room, the magistrates' reception hall, a more monumental aspect. At the rear were two small spaces, probably destined for the archives. The center of the western room was occupied by the rectangular altar of Hestia and formed the place of worship for the hearth of the city state. This building at Delos was a clear and harmonious realization of the theoretical plan of a Greek prytaneum.

Because of their architectural characteristics and their interior arrangements, it is impossible to distinguish between hypostyle and assembly halls, whether they were designed for religious use as at Eleusis, or for secular use as at Delos. In both cases, they consisted of huge rect-

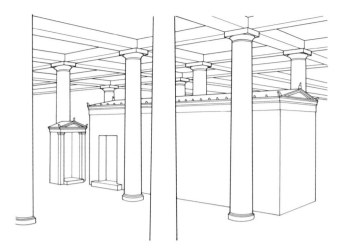

View of the Telesterion at Eleusis

angular halls, in some cases almost square. Inside, there were rows of columns arranged so as to leave a clear space in the center lit by a lantern. The entrance side was monumental in appearance.

Theaters

Theaters appear to have been the most purely original creations of civil architecture and their development continued into the Roman period. They were all the more original in that they stemmed from very rudimentary plans and represented a basic feature of the life of the city states. Theatrical performances developed from religious ceremonies and came to be closely integrated with Greek manners and customs. They became essential parts of life, so much so that the Athenian democracy initiated the 'theorikon,' or state entrance payment for every citizen, so that none need miss the performances. Thus, it is not surprising that the theater inspired some of the best productions of Greek literature and are of the most original types of building in their architecture.

Primitive theaters merely consisted of simple flat spaces, sometimes paved, but more often of beaten earth, where the choruses and dancers associated with the ceremonies of the cult of Dionysus could perform. An altar to the god stood in the center and this kept its place in the orchestras of later theaters. The spectators thronged round this dancing area, either on naturally sloping ground or on the wood stands represented in vase paintings. The first performances at Athens took place on the Angora, but a disaster caused by the collapse of the wood stands during a performance in 498 B.C. led to their transfer to the south side of the Acropolis where the audience was more advantageously accommodated on the gentle slopes at the foot of the cliff. The ground was leveled to form the orchestra or area for movement. This was the start of the theater whose remains still survive in this part of the Acropolis. At the edge of the flat area were probably a few flimsy buildings constructed of wood or canvas, known as 'skene,' a name suggesting that they were originally made of canvas. A small temple dedicated to Dionysus emphasized the second nature of the area. In the late 5th century, long porticoes and a few rows of stone seats initiated the architectural development which was to continue until the time of the Roman Empire when the sculptures on the foundation of the stage were attributed to the benficience of the Emperor Nero. Stone constructions, many of which were due to the great Athenian administrator Lycurgus, did not come into general use until the 4th century. At first, semicircular plans were not directly adopted; several theaters, notably the one at Syracuse, indicate arrangements primarily conceived to suit a rectangular plan similar to those used for assembly halls. In the end, however, the semicircular auditorium was generally adopted.

In the development of the Greek theater, its two main constituent features for a long period maintained their independence: these were the auditorium or 'cavea' containing the spectators, and the stage buildings reserved for the actors. The link between them was formed by the circular orchestra, the space used by the chorus which was originally the nodal point of the conception. The so-called 'skene' was a building set at a tangent to the orchestra, containing properties and boxes; its façade formed a back-cloth against or before which the highly simpli-fied decors were arranged. The chorus and actors used the orchestra in front of it. To begin with an actor was not separated from the chorus, but, later on, he was provided with a small wood platform, the 'logeion,' connected with the orchestra by a few steps. This was brought about by the nature of the plays themselves which required constant interchange between actors and chorus. It was not until the early 4th century that the logeion was raised to form a proper stage built of stone supported by Doric or Ionic columns; this arrangement survives in a good state of preservation at Priene and Segesta. Architectural unity of stage buildings and auditorium was never realized, however, in Greek theaters. The tiers of seats were built more or less in a semicircle, partially enclosing the orchestra until a point just beyond its diameter where they were stopped by a high retaining wall leaving a free passage known as the 'parodos' at each end; beyond this were the stage buildings. It was not until the late Hellenistic period, when the chorus had been given a reduced part in current plays clearly removed from the action and the individual actors, that stage buildings started to encroach on the orchestra so that if no longer formed a complete circle, and the ends of the seat tiers were linked to the skene by a monumental gate-way. This was the basis on which the Roman architects worked, using it as a model for their theater plans.

Aesthetic experiments in Greek theater buildings were centred on the plan of the cavea and its placing in a landscape setting. The principles of these experiments may be defined and understood by reference to the theaters at Pergamon, Priene and Ephesus in the East, Epidaurus and Dodona on the Greek mainland, and Segesta in the West. They aimed at achieving a delicately balanced harmony between the geometrical outline of the cavea and its placing in the landscape. In actual fact Greek theaters hardly ever had recourse to built up foundations; they were supported by natural slopes, the flanks of an acropolis or the folds of hills and submitted themselves to the lines and movements of the ground. They were also planned with geometrical exactitude as has been discovered at Epidaurus and other sites suffici-ently well preserved to allow detailed study. The curve of the cavea is slightly irregular; it exceeds an exact semicircle and opens out at the ends to permit interior movement; it is designed with a single radius directed from a single center. As a rule, the middle section has its corresponding center in the center of the orchestra, but the end blocks have a more open circumference with longer radii extending from centers which do not correspond with that of the orchestra. None of these details is obvious to the eye and they can only be recognized by measuring; like the optical corrections of the Parthenon, they help to turn the theaters of Dodona, Epidaurus and Segesta into splendid geometrical compositions perfectly set in land-scapes seemingly designed to receive them. Nevertheless, this subordination of a theater to the amenities of a site did not preclude its orientation to the south wherever possible. It also explains why theaters were seldom included with other buildings to form a general composi-tion. It was too difficult to integrate them in town plans.

Plates

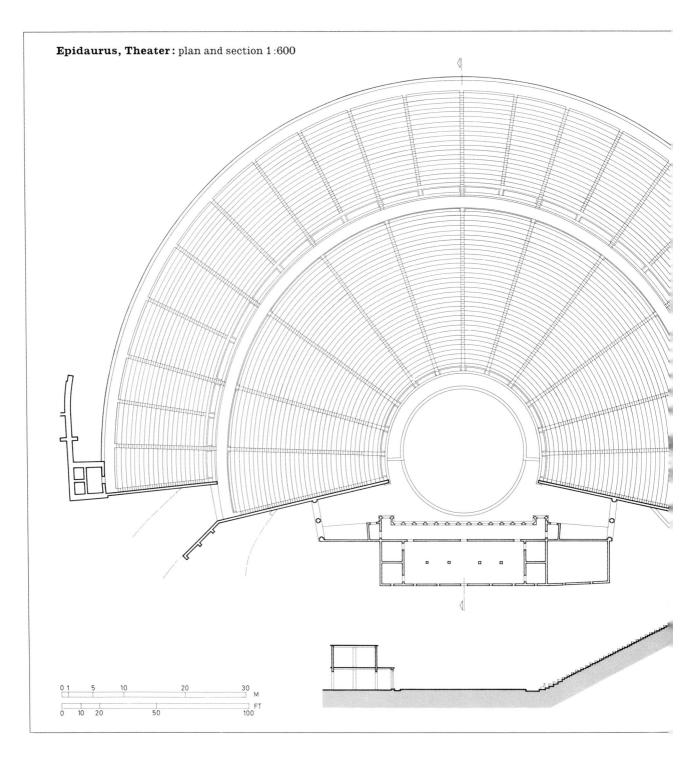

Epidaurus, Theater: plan and section 1:600

0 1   5   10   20   30 M
0   10 20   50   100 FT

Detail of proscenium, elevation and plan 1:100; Detail of seats 1:20

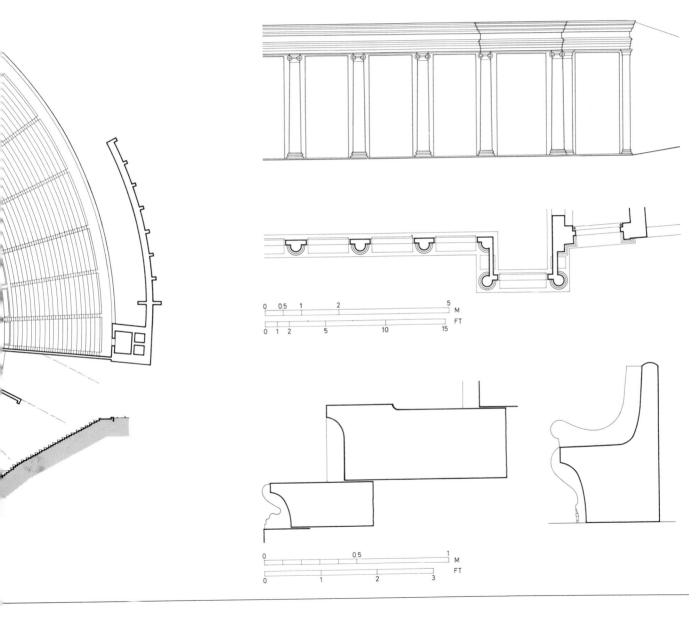

0   0.5   1   2   5   M
                                                           FT
0   1 2   5   10   15

0   0.5   1   M
                                                    FT
0   1   2   3

Notes

Priene and Pythius

Priene is famous on two counts in the architectural history of Greece: its town plan and the buildings executed by Pythius, one of the master architects of the second half of the 4th century. At the start of the century the inhabitants of Priene lived in a city constantly swamped in mud from the river Meander. Therefore, they decided to found a new town on a terrace overlooking the valley; this was backed by a formidable rock wall forming an acropolis. The plan which they adopted was uncompromisingly rectilinear, notwithstanding the somewhat roughly sloping ground which turned the streets into long stepped ramps. For the town planner, Priene represents a first-class working drawing. The agora occupies a prominent position together with the adjacent buildings which include the Bouleuterion and the magnificent terrace of the temple of Athene, Pythius's masterpiece. Many years later Vitruvius still used to consult one of his treatises commending the Ionic order which he had used to such brilliant effect in this temple. As module he chose the side of the plinth supporting the Ionic columns of the peristyle: all the dimensions of the plans were fixed in accordance with this. The rhythm of the colonnade, the proportions of the pronaos, the length and positioning of the cella walls were all integrated within the prescribed pattern.

Epidaurus and Polycleitus the Younger

The sanctuary of Asclepius at Epidaurus was decorated with painted terracotta and set in the midst of a number of buildings constructed of tufa or limestone. It included two masterpieces: the Thymela or tholos and its theater, both, according to Pausanias, the work of an Argive architect who belonged to the great Polycleitus family which provided the workshops with master sculptors and architects throughout the 5th and 4th centuries. The attribution of these two buildings to a single architect famed for his skill in working out proportions is now questioned. It is, indeed, possible that Pausanias and other guides may have confused him with the master sculptor of the 5th century. Nevertheless, whether the architects are anonymous or not, they deserve mention for the strength of their conception, their taste for innovation, feeling for architectural decoration and outstanding skill in harmonious, geometrical composition.

Dodona and its oracle

Dodona, so long isolated in the mountains of Epirus, has not attained the reputation of the great classical sites. Now, however, the originality of the oracle of Zeus, the beauty of the landscape and the importance of the buildings are attracting attention to the excavations of the site. The theater, one of the most forceful examples of this type of building in Greece, is distinguished by its great butresses and the sharp outline of its stage buildings, with their alternate rusticated and pitted curved blocks. Dodona and the Necromanteion of Ephyrus occupy a key position both in the history of religious ideas and oracles and in the development of architectural design.

The agora at Athens

The architectural development of the agora reflects the formation of the democratic city state. It enables us to follow its history from the first building contemporary with the reforms of Solon at the beginning of the 6th century B.C. until the last days of the ancient city over ten centuries later when it was sacked by the barbarian invaders. Many original formulae were tried out on the site where each main division of the city's life – political, religious and commercial – created and developed the individual buildings they required.

The Stoa of Attalus unites its political and practical aims in its lavish proportions, clearly defined forms and vast interior space. The kings of Pergamon here achieved an architectural composition that was a special feature of Greek cities but was outdated in their own capital. There is no better illustration of the feeling for Hellenism acquired and practised by the Attalids.

The mausoleum of Theron

This monument, set on a quadrangular base supporting a storey decorated with an architectural motif, belongs to an original series of funerary buildings stemming from the 5th century tombs at Cnidus. They are typified by the 'Nereid Monument' at Xanthus, expand into the famous Mausoleum at Halicarnassus, and are finally found scattered all along the Mediterranean littoral in Syria, Africa, Italy and Gaul.

169

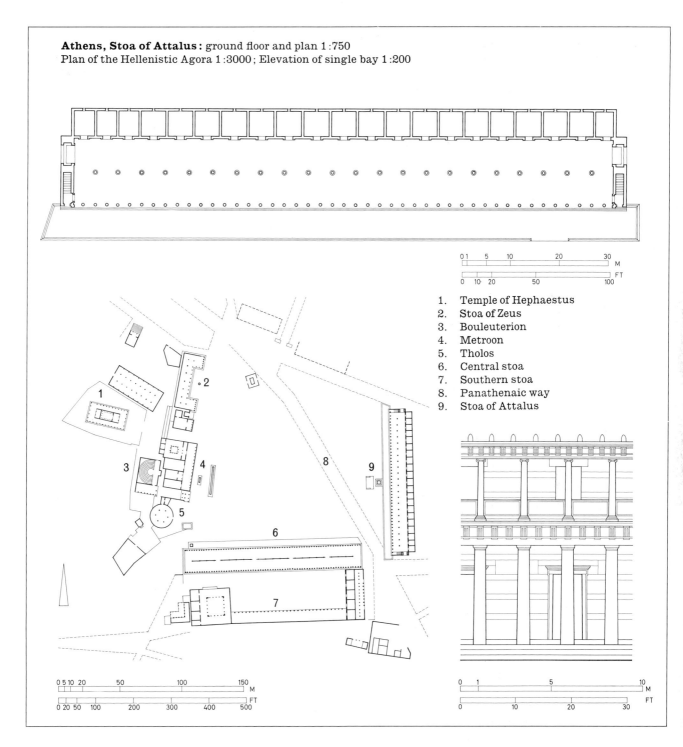

Athens, Stoa of Attalus: ground floor and plan 1:750
Plan of the Hellenistic Agora 1:3000; Elevation of single bay 1:200

1. Temple of Hephaestus
2. Stoa of Zeus
3. Bouleuterion
4. Metroon
5. Tholos
6. Central stoa
7. Southern stoa
8. Panathenaic way
9. Stoa of Attalus

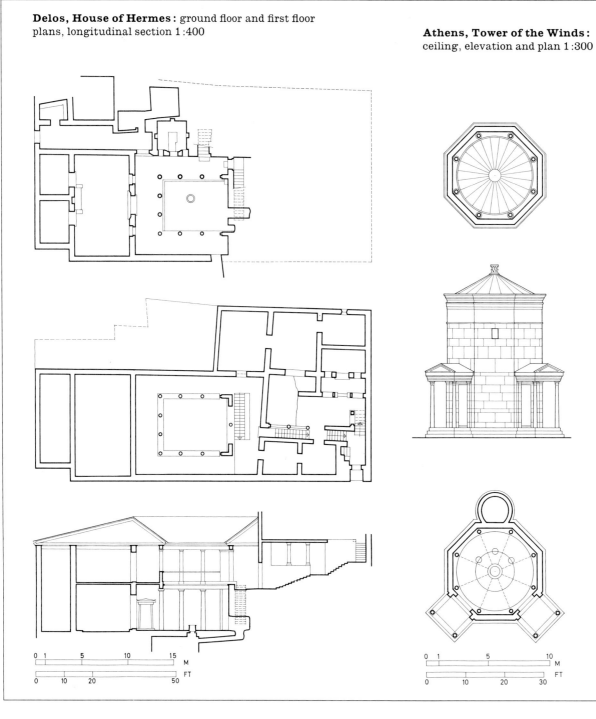

Delos, House of Hermes: ground floor and first floor plans, longitudinal section 1:400

Athens, Tower of the Winds: ceiling, elevation and plan 1:300

0 1   5   10   15   M

0   10   20   50 FT

0 1   5   10   M

0   10   20   30 FT

5. Evolution and Development of the Principles of Architectural Composition

We must now investigate the problem of architectural composition. So far we have studied individual buildings, their plans, constructions and masses without any consideration of their relationship to neighboring structures, with which they were sometimes integrated. This problem was not fully considered until the Hellenistic period, but, though the creative dynamism of the archaic period almost wholly ignored it, the architects of the 5th and 4th centuries were driven to establish the first principles of architectural composition by the introduction of two new features into their sphere of work — one aesthetic, the other a blend of philosophy and politics.

First attempts at architectural composition

The mid-fifth century witnessed an important event in the art of drawing: the discovery of perspective by the painter and decorator, Agatharchus of Samos. This was not, however, the mathematical perspective used in the study of spatial geometery and based on the choice of a point from which all geometrical figures are seen and drawn from an identical angle whose summit coincides with the determined point. It was a wider application of this principle to the art of painting where it was the convention to portray buildings and architectural decoration by a system of fleeting lines giving an illusion of depth. The painters Polygnotus and Nicon had already experimented in this direction. Agatharchus was responsible for the decoration of the house of Alcibiades (which caused a great scandal among his contemporaries), and produced some theater backcloths in which he applied his new methods to landscape and architectural views, accentuating effects by chiaroscuro and contrasting colors.

Architects were influenced by this progress in painting and became more sensitive to the

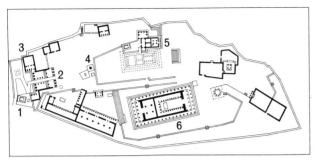

Plan of the Acropolis at Athens

1. Temple of Athena Nike
2. Propylaea
3. Pinakotheke
4. Statue of Athena
5. Erechtheum
6. Parthenon

within the peristyle. Finally, the impressive mass of the façade was emphasized by a wide ramp of curved monumental steps similar to the one which enlivened the temple steps and was echoed in the frieze and architrave.

Mnesicles, the architect of the Propylaea, was possibly even more sensitive to the relationship of buildings to one another. His task was complicated by the lie of the ground, the needs imposed by earlier buildings and proprietary

Plan of the city of Miletus

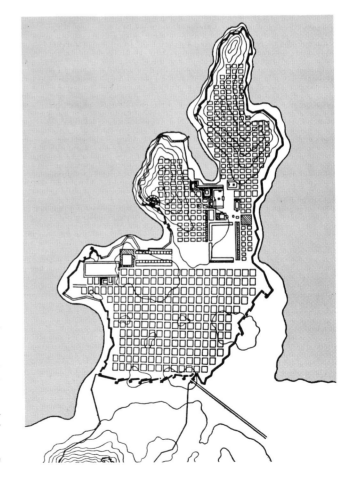

plastic quality of individual buildings, to the relationship between them and their reciprocal setting in space. Evidence of this may be found in work carried out on the Acropolis under the direction of Phidias who started his career as a painter in the studio of Polygnotus. First we may see how the Parthenon revealed itself to the visitor emerging from the Propylaea. The most important building on the Acropolis was hidden from sight by the walls of the sanctuary of Athena Brauronia, and it was necessary to pass through another propylon into an interior court to confront the full splendor of the west façade and the impressive north flank of the temple. Moreover, Ictinus did not wish the mass of the building to be seen head on, but from an angle, so that it could be fully revealed in three dimensions. More exact investigations have shown that, from the standpoint enforced on the pilgrim setting eyes on the great temple of Athena for the first time, the sight lines were so calculated that the building could be absorbed in a single glance. Horizontally, the lines containing the eight columns of the façade describe an angle of 45 degrees, the angle of normal vision. Vertically, the eye travels successively over three decorative zones: the pediments, the exterior metopes, and the processional frieze

174

rights. Nevertheless, he succeeded in placing his building with due regard to the orientation of the Parthenon which was completed just as he started work. The longitudinal axis of the Propylaea is almost at right angles to that of the Parthenon. The lengths of the two buildings (222.6 feet and 221.8 feet) correspond and their modules are similar. A subtle volumetric relationship was thus established between the building forming a frontispiece to the Acropolis and the chief temple of the group.

Even before Pericles had inspired and set in motion the building programs for the Acropolis, new ideas on town plans had come into being; these were to exercise their influence on architectural compositions set up in town centers, especially in the following century. These innovations may generally be attributed to Hippodamus of Miletus, political theorist, philosopher, architect and town-planner. His ideas and theories exerted considerable influence as may be seen from the way in which they were applied, first in his native Miletus and later at Piraeus.

Despite the probability that he played no practical part in building, he disclosed the principles of a functional town plan to the architects of Greece. Its features, defined and arranged in relation to their functions – business, religious, political, and so on– were then outlined on the ground by a system of boundaries whose principles have been revealed by inscriptions discovered at Piraeus. The first group of boundary stones outlined the built-up zones reserved for business installations, military and public buildings. The exact positions of the buildings are known thanks to a second series of inscriptions of later date. From them we may grasp the principle of this division of urban land. The whole site was first divided into districts separated by zones devoted to public services including the harbor, the agora, arsenals and

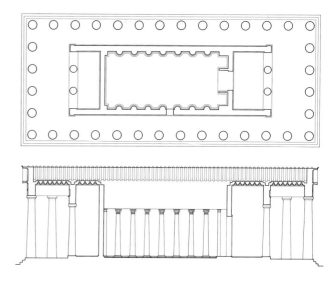

Plan and longitudinal section of the temple at Tegea

temples. The exact placing of each building was then worked out in relation to streets and neighboring structures.

In this way the idea of the interrelation of buildings was brought home to architects by means of a town-planning system whose good and bad points may be seen at Miletus.

The era of individual experiment

Between two periods when Greek architecture was mainly directed towards relatively uniform schemes there appeared a tendency to adopt more individual characteristics; this brought about the development of the inheritance of the classic period and paved the way for the large-scale plans of Hellenistic towns. The architectural creations of this transitional period, which occupied part of the 4th century, reveal apparently contradictory attitudes. Sometimes there is clearly a somewhat restrained respect for the proportions and forms of the classic period. But behind these principles, changes were taking place, stemming from a new spirit which abolished taboos and standards.

The conquest of interior space

This spirit of innovation first made itself felt in the arrangement of interior space which formed the basis of the original characteristics of 4th century buildings. An early example of these manifestations may be found in the Parthenon where, as has already been noted, it was caused by the collaboration of a sculptor and an architect. A similar phenomenon brought about the development of this tendency and is most clearly exemplified by the temple at Tegea, the work of Scopas who was also both architect and sculptor. The old Temple of Athena Alea was destroyed by fire in 393 B.C., and, towards the middle of the century or shortly before, the inhabitants of Tegea commissioned Scopas to rebuild it and provide it with sculptured decora-

Cella of the temple of Apollo at Bassae

tion. From outside the temple appears to have no original features. Once inside the cella, however, all this is changed.

In the first place, the proportions of the interior were remarkable. Scopas succeeded in creating a magnificent space, freeing it from the heavy interior colonnades which Ictinus had been forced to keep at the Parthenon because of the long spans; the architect of the temple at Bassae had also not been able to dispense with them, though he applied an interior order to the ends of small walls bordering niches which could not be used. From this resulted a great complication in the system of the interior capitals and the arrangement of the ceiling. The cella at Bassae remained cluttered up, lacking space and impulse. Scopas adopted a cleaner, more elegant solution. He placed his interior order against the walls in the form of Corinthian half-columns surmounted by Ionic pilasters. The latter were ignored when the temple was first published, but their presence has been confirmed by newly identified fragments and by comparison with the temple at Nemea which was a copy of Tegea. The lofty walls were divided into panels and enlivened by the applied order; Scopas also placed abundant decoration at various levels. The Corinthian capitals, with their forceful vegetable ornament, were designed by a sculptor, and are markedly different from the first timid attempts to realize the order at Bassae and in the tholos at Delphi; they are also more luxuriant and more strongly carved than the capitals of the tholos at Epidaurus. The Corinthian order is crowned by an architrave decorated with egg-and-dart. Above this it remains to restore the Ionic pilasters which were also surmounted by a sculptured course.

The successes of Scopas at Tegea had other still more important consequences. He had helped to breach some of the principles of classic architecture and open new avenues heralding the spirit of the Hellenistic period. With this mixing of different styles in a single building, came the start of the development of applied orders which were to become of such vital importance in Roman architecture. The combination of styles in a single building was related to requirements emphasized by Mnesicles in the Propylaea on the Acropolis. The slim proportions of Ionic columns forced them to be used in interior orders where it was necessary to support a ceiling at a higher level than that of the Doric frieze on the exterior. This is, in fact, what Mnesicles did in the central block of his building. Other architects followed him, with the result that all the great stoas combined the two orders: their colonnaded façades were Doric, but inside, slim Ionic columns supported the timber ridge-roof. For the same reason, the Ionic order was used within the temple at Bassae. At Tegea, Scopas went one step further by experimenting with decoration in addition to purely architectural considerations.

At Epidaurus, too, is preserved what is probably the richest of the creations inspired by this taste for architectural decoration indulged by the sculptor-architects of the 4th century. This is the tholos, or Thymela, attributed by Pausanias to an artist member of the Polycleitus family. It was not mere chance that the same period witnessed the development at Delphi, Epidaurus and Olympia of the finest circular plan buildings left us by Greek architecture. Their use has been the subject of continual discussion, but, here we are only concerned with their architectural significance. The tholos at Delphi, the oldest of the three, is also the most classic in style. Its inspiration comes directly from the architects of Attica and it is conceived on a purely mathematical basis; the cutting and shape of the stones, the positioning of columns, courses and walls are all determined by a strict geometrical composition. Nevertheless, the style of the Doric colonnade is

already lightened by a scrolled gutter and the base of the walls is lined with a carved motif of water-leaves introducing a note of fantasy. The interior was decorated with plain Corinthian half-columns. The significance of the tholos at Delphi, as with the great Attic monuments of the 5th century, lies in the correct balance of its proportions, the precise use and quality of its materials, its constructional technique, and strict mathematical order.

The tholos at Epidaurus makes a completely different aesthetic effect with its riotous surge of decoration. It is as much the work of a decorator as of an architect due to the basic idea behind the plan, the variety and interplay of materials, and rich decoration.

The plan itself has decorative significance and, by different means, expressed the same principle put into practice by Scopas in the Temple of Athena at Tegea. The exterior was ringed by a slim, light Doric colonnade which enclosed the cella wall. This, with its molded pedestal and a course carved with floral motifs between the orthostats and the ordinary courses, formed a complete break with the geometrical severity of the Doric wall. Inside, a very fine Corinthian colonnade repeated and accentuated the circular plan and an experiment in polychromy resulted in an interplay of materials – above and below each course was set black marble corresponding to the black and white lozenges of the paving. It remains to imagine a painted wood ceiling, probably dome-shaped, to gain an idea of the complex interplay of the materials: tufa encased in stucco, Pentelic marble, and black marble.

Experiments in decoration enlivened the exterior Doric frieze where the metopes were ornamented with an unusual motif. Each one displayed a rosette with little lotus flowers set in the cavaties. Looking upwards from the foot of the wall to the peristyle ceiling, the eye was attracted by richer and ever more crowded decorations. The plinth of the wall was decorated with a plain ogee molding, while a projecting intermediary course had a motif of palmettes and lotus flowers emerging from a calyx formed of three acanthus leaves. The peristyle ceiling was composed of marble slabs, the soffits ornamented with trapezoidal, nearly square, coffers. These coffers were filled with rosettes and the divisions framing them were occupied by scrolls of acanthus and fleurs-de-lis linked with garlands of pearls and chaplets. The door also constituted a masterpiece of 4th century decorative art thanks to the association and interplay of similar motifs emphasized by the rosettes ornamenting the posts. Inside the cella the Corinthian order came into its own.

The development of domestic architecture

The various tendencies revealed through an examination of the architectural creations of the period, especially the interest in interior arrangements and the increased part played by decoration explain why there was also a development of domestic architecture at the same time. It also answered the evolution of political and social ideas which, till then, had ensured the predominance of civil and religious architecture. The needs of the state and the community prevailed over the leisure and aspirations of private individuals. In the 4th century, the weakening of political links together with the increase of professional activities brought about the liberation of the individual and led to an interest in a more personal background.

During the archaic and classic periods there was a marked absence of any noteworthy domestic architecture. Even in 5th century Athens, a city which had become a school for the whole of Greece and mistress of all the arts,

engaged on the building program on the Acropolis, house types had not changed since the archaic period; there had been scarcely any enlargement on the rudimentary plan of primitive times. An unplanned group of rooms and halls huddled round an open space which eventually turned into a courtyard. They were heaped against one another in the most irregular shapes; the rules for builders of houses certainly did not include respect for right angles. In the following century, however, Xenophon formulated principles for the design of a comfortable house. It had to be cool in summer and warm in winter. Houses facing south had the sun in winter, and in summer were in shade.

Excavations at Olynthus in northern Greece have revealed a type of house exactly corresponding to Xenophon's requirements. It is arranged round a courtyard which takes up the southern section of the group of buildings. The north side of the court is bordered by the main wing of the house consisting of a single storey. The ground-floor or principal rooms open on to a colonnade. On the south side of the court are lower rooms – studios, entrance and shops communicating with the street. A remarkable and almost modern feature of this house at Olynthus is the arrangement of the purely functional spaces of kitchen and bathroom. There is one large room, 16.5 to 28 feet long and 13 to 16.2 feet wide, which may be identified as a kitchen from the presence of a hearth and two smaller rooms one of which seems to have been a bathroom provided with a small bath resembling a modern slipper bath. There are even surviving inscriptions relating to the prices of similar houses.

House plans at Priene were somewhat different. The main room was based on the megaron and opened on to the court through a vestibule. A corridor whose length varied according to the position of the house in the block led from the street to the courtyard. The other two sides of the court were occupied by two or more small rooms. At the edges of the principal streets, a strip of ground about twenty feet wide was reserved for the siting of shops independent of the houses behind them. The latter were reached by passages set between groups of three or four shops.

Any attempt to reconstruct the general lines and appearance of a Greek house will meet with surest success at Delos in the maze of twisting streets leading to the theater. The state of preservation, the quality of floors and mosaics, and recent restorations provide a firm base for a reconstruction.

The first surprise is the amazing variety of forms and compositions. It is impossible to provide an adequate explanation for this extra-ordinary overlapping of plans and buildings. The courtyard was the one stable feature in all this variety. Whether the house was large or small, there was always either a small court with rough paving or a lavish courtyard with a marble peristyle and a mosaic floor. The rooms surrounded two or three sides, but there was no common form of orientation. The main reception room and its ancillaries, however, were preferably situated on the north side, opening to the south. Some colonnades were widely developed and included a raised storey on the north front, thus ensuring twice as much sun; this was known as the Rhodian type of colonnade. Below the courtyard there was usually a large tank covered with great slabs resting on arches of masonry. The floor, like those of the main reception rooms, was decorated with fine mosaics; indeed the most splendid examples of Hellenistic mosaics must be credited to the taste of the rich connoisseurs of Delos.

The architects made good use of the uneven

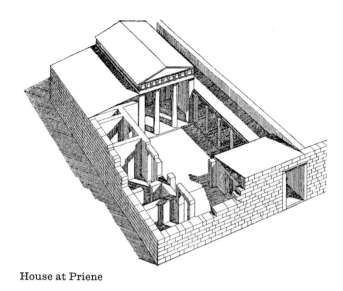

House at Priene

nature of the site so as to serve the different storeys of their houses. The best example of this is the House of Hermes. The same house also offers another characteristic – a systematic investigation into the union of statuary with the architectural plan. The north wall of the large ground-floor reception room was clearly designed to serve as a background to the statue of the master of the house, and the staircases to the upper floors seem to have been thrown off center so that the composition of statue and niches could be seen from the two upper landings through the wide arch linking the room with the peristyle court.

Great architectural compositions and Greek town-planning

We have already noted the birth of functional town-planning at Miletus and its application at the Piraeus. It formed a constant source of inspiration in the great drive to create cities after the conquests of Alexander and constituted a basic feature of the Hellenization of the eastern world.

The orthogonal plan was based on the geometrical division of a site and had as module the shape and dimensions of the 'insula' or block. Houses and public buildings were integrated in these defined areas which formed the basic elements of the plan; the regular arrangement of agoras, temples, and gymnasia was governed by the proportions of the block. This resulted in architectural composition being reduced to a unanimous adaptation to the linear movement of the plan. The massive outlines of buildings had to be subjected to the structure of the grid, so that their individuality was toned down. In these circumstances, the street could not develop on a wide scale nor could it be accorded independent architectural decoration. Moreover, its proportions were on a reduced scale, its width varying from 13 to 23 feet and its rectilinear outline did not suit monumental perspectives. It was really no more than a passage bordered by a monotonous line of house fronts, although these houses were centrally planned round their interior courtyards. There were no large entrances to the street and, at Priene, the only form of decoration seems to have been the massive masonry of the foundations. Priene provides a concise example of the possibilities and limitations of this plan. Paradoxically applied to an extremely uneven, mountainous site, the cross streets were often transformed into staircases so that methods of transport were limited to beasts of burden. It was difficult to insert large buildings into the network, even though they were integrated in the orthogonal plan and corresponded to a whole number of blocks. The Agora, the Temple of Athena on its terrace, and the Gymnasium all tended to enlarge themselves to the detriment of the streets; it is quite likely that the temple blocked the way to the west so that the street of Athena could not reach the rampart.

Plan of the city of Priene

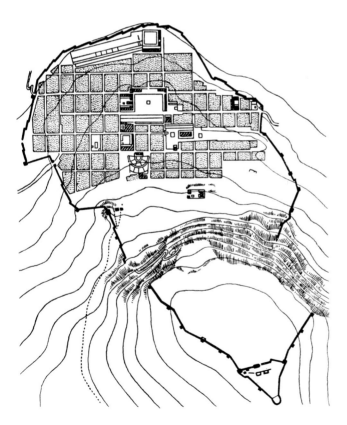

At about the same time, the citizens of Magnesia, who were in process of changing the site of their city, created some highly significant deviations from the orthogonal plan. They regrouped themselves around the Temple of Artemis Leukophryene which was positioned in accordance with a ritualistic orientation. Excavations have revealed beyond all doubt that the basic plan was on the grid, but the monumental mass of the temple maintained its independence; only the agora which was associated with it was incorporated in the plan. This exactly covers the area of six blocks and is linked with one of the main streets; the overall composition, however, reveals experiments in diagonal perspective and breaks the monotony of the right-angled pattern.

The credit for developing these new tendencies and for introducing monumentality and a feeling for related masses into the planning of cities must be offered to the Pergamene architects. In order to define the nature of their originality, we must first examine the characteristics of the site which they used to best advantage, finally developing their predecessors' feeling for landscape and siting buildings in perfect harmony with the natural lines of the landscape. The town was set on an outcrop of dark trachyte forming a spur on the south side of the high massif of the Madaras-Dagh, the ancient Pindasus, between deep valleys hollowed by two tributaries of the Caicus, the Selinus on the west and the Ketius on the east. The summit of the acropolis rises 1,100 feet above sea level and 900 feet above the surrounding plain, and forms a kind of platform slightly tilted towards the west and descending in a series of landings towards the south. A monumental building was set on each of these landings and the entire composition resembled an open fan with the theater forming the central pivot. On the topmost level were storehouses, then the Trajeneum and, 66 feet below, the esplanade of the Temple of Athena.

This terrace was eventually widened, allowing royal palaces to be built towards the east. Simultaneously, the western arc of the fan was continued over two more landings containing the great altar, famous for its sculptures, 83 feet below the Temple of Athena and finally, 50 feet further down, the agora which formed the monumental entrance to a composition not realized as a single project but resulting from a succession of cleverly linked programs. The more gradual southern slopes were covered with houses whose continuity was broken here and there by terraces supporting sanctuaries like the Temple of Demeter or architectural compositions such as gymnasia, which stretched towards the main entrance gate in the south-eastern section of the ramparts.

It is worth noting that all the terraces, including those of the acropolis, maintained their functional and architectural independence. The agora, which formed the starting point of the main axis, constituted the principal square. In this royal city, however, its political and administrative functions were reduced, for power was concentrated in the palaces set on the acropolis behind the temples. Originally these terraces had not been designed to intercommunicate; links were later established between them by means of secondary staircases or of subsidiary passages arranged where there were gaps between the main buildings. This is sure proof that none of the architects was first provided with an overall plan; the ultimate unity was more organic and lively.

Also worth investigating are the principles and means employed by the architects serving the Attalids, especially Attalus I and Eumenes II, the two great builders of the dynasty, to realize the unity of work whose development extended over a century or more. On analysis, it appears that one basic principle was applied: submission to the nature of the ground and the adaptation of architecture to the site. In this tormented landscape the outline of the walls and the lines of streets assumed great flexibility; they scaled slopes or wound round them with a remarkable suppleness of line.

This method, however, gave rise to more audacious schemes involving the enlargement and regularization of the terraces. They became a basic constructional feature molded into shape along with the landscape. To enlarge their area, buildings were set on the extreme edges of the terraces, and sometimes extended beyond them. The inner sides of stoas planted against the rising slope were buried in the rock and their outer edges were supported

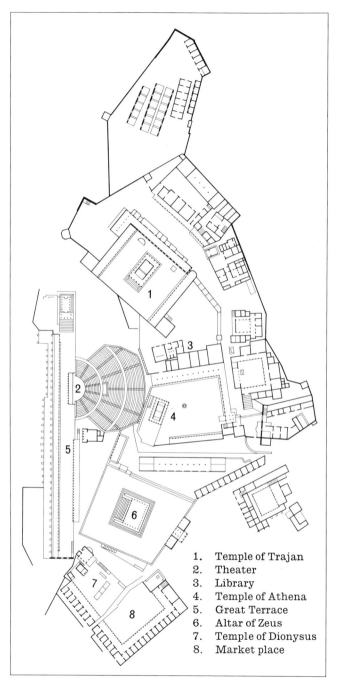

on a level lower than that of the terrace so that the landscape became an integral part of the building. The perfect illustration of this type of constructional procedure lies in the massive blocks supporting the stoa, 732.6 feet long, which borders the terrace of the theater and serves as a base line unifying the concentric movement of the various landings of the acropolis. The foundations first describe several horizontal lines stressing the general movement of the ground by a succession of three super-imposed terraces. These lines are also cut vertically by a regular arrangement of massive, projecting buttresses which extend from the

Plan of the Agora at Pergamon

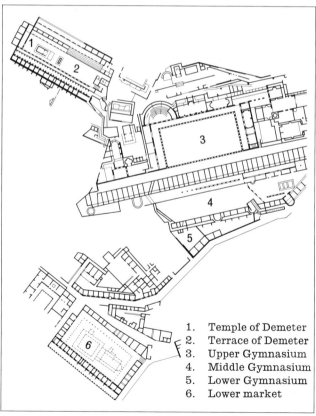

1. Temple of Trajan
2. Theater
3. Library
4. Temple of Athena
5. Great Terrace
6. Altar of Zeus
7. Temple of Dionysus
8. Market place

Plan of the Acropolis at Pergamon

1. Temple of Demeter
2. Terrace of Demeter
3. Upper Gymnasium
4. Middle Gymnasium
5. Lower Gymnasium
6. Lower market

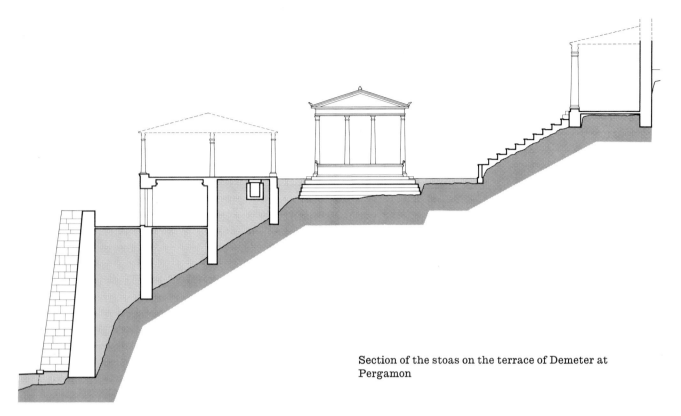

Section of the stoas on the terrace of Demeter at Pergamon

lowest level to the top-most colonnade. In this way, it is possible to pass from the lines of the landscape to the buildings by a series of skilfully calculated transitions.

These compositional procedures serve to explain the changes made by Pergamene architects in the types and forms of the traditional repertory. To consolidate the terraces and form a background to their buildings, they had recourse to porticoes and colonnades. They did not hesitate to draw these out to considerable lengths and increase their height to two or three storeys, making them harmonize with the landscape background.

Stoas, public buildings, and private houses were laid out so as to benefit from differences in level and use was made of storeys corresponding

to each terrace. The same type of portico was employed in the two agoras at the entrance to the acropolis and in the lower town, in the gymnasia, the Temple of Athena, and the theater. The upper storey with a colonnade was sometimes open on two sides, corresponded to the level of the terrace, and provided a free view over the surrounding countryside. The lower levels were occupied by basement rooms serving as workshops, shops and storerooms, and established links with the lower terraces.

The Pergamene architects made use of traditional formulae but also introduced into the history of Greek architecture and town-planning a novel conception: a feeling for monumentality and the integration of landscape and architecture. Without abolishing basic principles they created an architecture which stressed volumes and in which the relationship of masses and the search for monumental effect resulted from a renewed aesthetic ideal. This type of architecture expressed an idea quite different from that behind the architecture of earlier Greek city states. Pergamon was a royal city, made by princes for their own pleasure; as such, it had to express their power and glory. This was a fertile innovation which allowed Greek architecture to adapt itself to new historical and economic circumstances in the Greco-Roman world, very different from the restricted background of the Greek city states.

The part played by the street

The most immediate consequence of Pergamon was the importance of monumental masses which broke the rigidity of the traditional town plan. This helped to create a new aesthetic based on the street. In cities of the classic period, streets were no more than narrow corridors devoid of any form of decoration. In the late Hellenistic period, however, they underwent a series of radical transformations. First of all they were expanded into avenues often over 60 feet wide. The long colonnades which had surrounded the terraces at Pergamon now frequently bordered the entire length of a main thoroughfare. The large planned cities of Asia Minor and Syria – Ephesus, Perga, Side, Antioch, and Apameia – were all provided with these colonnaded avenues which were repeated, whenever possible, in the ancient cities of Greece during the imperial period. Corinth is a good example of this. The unfolding of these long colonnades resulted however, in a monotonous effect and, at this point, experiments with perspective effects were completed by the introduction of monumental masses to break up or close architectural compositions. A basic principle of the aesthetics of town-planning is to close the perspective of a street with a monumental mass and this was the part allocated to

gates, triumphal arches and tetra-pylons of various forms. A similar role was played by columns, isolated or in groups, used as supports for commemorative statues. This decorative theme, frequently employed in townscapes of the imperial period, was probably borrowed from the traditional repertory. Ever since the archaic period, isolated and later coupled columns had been used to support groups of statuary decorating Greek temples.

This special example enables us to grasp the radical law which changed and transformed the Hellenic heritage in later architectural history. The forms of Hellenic architecture originated and developed within the well defined, restricted framework of the Greek city state and preserved their own individual characteristics based on a preoccupation with functional values and more or less excluding aesthetic experiments. For a long time they remained anchored to the scale of the men and communities who had created them, strictly linked with their original spiritual and material circumstances. Later on, however, came a new age when the political, social and economic structure shattered the traditional framework.

These old forms were no longer regarded as entities, but became features of much vaster, monumental compositions. They became no more than pieces of a whole in which a taste for composition and investigation into the value of decoration had got the better of strict constructional necessities which supplied each form with an individual personality and made perfect adaptation to function the sole criterion of architectural significance.

Chronological Table

Dates	Historical Events	Buildings
1050	End of the Dorian invasions	
900	Creation of the Ionian Confederation	Temple with apsidal plan
	Development of the geometrical style	Temple Artemis Orthia at Sparta
		Megaron B at Thermum
800		First Heraeum at Samos
776	Foundation of the Olympic Games	First Heraeum at Olympia
734	Foundation of Syracuse	First temple of Argive Hera
		(Possibly first peripteral plan)
600	Foundation of Marseilles	Temple at Corfu
		Second Heraeum at Samos
580–60		Temple of Apollo at Syracuse
		Treasury of Gela at Olympia
		Temple at Thermum
561—60	Peisistratus seizes power at Athens; death of Solon	Temple by Rhoecus at Samos
550–540	New period of tyranny of Peisistratus	Temple C, Selinunte
	Period of tyrannies in Greek city states	Temple of Apollo, Corinth
		Temple at Assos
		Temple D, Selinunte
530–500	Cleisthenes succeeds at Athens	Ionian Treasuries, Delphi
	End of the tyrants	Temple of Polycrates, Samos
		Temple of Athena on the Acropolis
		Temple of the Alcmaeonids, Delphi
		Temple of Aphaia, Aegina
		Work started on the Olympeium at Athens
		'Basilica' at Paestum

Dates	Historical Events	Buildings
490–480	Persian wars Battles of Marathon (490), Salamis (480), Plataea (479)	Treasury of the Athenians, Delphi Temple of Athena, Paestum First Parthenon Temple of Athena Pronaia, Delphi Temple of Athena, Syracuse Temple at Himera Temple G, Selinunte
480–450	Development of the Athenian Empire Extension of Carthaginian power in the west	Outline of plan for Miletus Temple of Zeus, Olympia Tholos in the Agora at Athens Plan for the Piraeus Temple of Hera, Agrigento Olympeium, Agrigento Temples E and F, Selinunte
448–430	Pericles at the height of his power in Athens Attempts by Pericles to form a panhellenic federation Development of the Sophoclean drama	Parthenon and Propylaea Temple of Hephaestus at Athens Temple at Sunium Temple at Rhamnus Temple of Poseidon, Paestum Temples A and O, Selinunte Ionic temple, Locri Temple by the Ilissus
430–400	Peloponnesian War between Sparta and Athens Success of the comedies of Aristophanes	Temple of Athena Nike Erechtheum Architectural development of the Athens Agora Temple of Concord, Agrigento Temple of Apollo, Delos Temple at Segesta Temple of Hera, Argos Temple at Bassae Telesterion, Eleusis

Dates	Historical Events	Buildings
390–380	Struggle for hegemony between Thebes, Athens and Sparta	Temple of Asclepius at Epidaurus
360–350	Development of Persian satrapies in Asia Minor	Rebuilding of the Temple of Artemis at Ephesus
		Rebuilding of the Temple of Cybele at Sardeis
		Building started at Labranda
		Tholos at Delphi
		Plan for Priene
350–330	Rivalry between Athens and the power of Macedon	Temple of Athene, Tegea
	336: Death of Philip and succession of Alexander	Temple of Zeus, Nemea
		4th century Temple of Apollo, Delphi
		Mausoleum of Halicarnassus
		Temple of Zeus, Stratus
		Tholos at Epidaurus
		Theater of Dionysus, Athens
		Temple of Athena, Priene
323	Death of Alexander	Metroon at Olympia
		Theater at Epidaurus
		Theater at Alinda
		Monument of Nikias, Athens
		Plan for Alexandria
300–250	Development of Hellenistic monarchies particularly the Attalids at Pergamon and the Lagids at Alexandria	Plan for Pergamon
		Temple of Athena, Pergamon
		Necromanteion, Ephyra
		Theater at Dodona
		Temple of Apollo, Clarus
		Work started on the temple at Didyma
		Temple of Mesa (Lesbos)
250–150	Struggles between the Hellenistic monarchies, and the start of the Roman conquest	Large-scale development of Pergamon
		Temple of Artemis at Magnesia
		Agoras at Miletus
		Agora at Magnesia
		Stoa of Attalus, Athens
		Urban developments on Delos

Bibliography

General Works

Choisy, A.
Histoire de l'Architecture. T. I, L'Antiquité. Paris, 1899

Dinsmoor, W. B.
The Architecture of Ancient Greece, London, 1950

Durm, J.
Handbuch der Architektur. Die Baukunst der Griechen, 3rd ed. Leipzig, 1910

Lawrence, A. W.
The Greek Architecture, London, 1957

Martin, R.
L'Urbanisme dans la Grèce antique. Paris, 1956

Martin, R.
Manuel d'architecture grecque. T. I, Matériaux et techniques. Paris, 1965

Noack, F.
Baukunst des Altertums. Berlin, 1910

Perrot, G. et Chipiez, C.
Histoire de l'art. T. VI, Le temple grec. Paris, 1894

Robertson, D. S.
Handbook of Greek Roman Architecture, 2nd ed. Cambridge, 1943

Styles and forms

Andrae, W.
Die ionische Säule, Bauform oder Symbol? Berlin, 1933

Braun-Vogelstein, J.
Die ionische Säule (Jahrbuch des Deutschen Archaeol. Inst., XXXV, 1920)

Buren, E. D. von
Archaic Fictile Revetments in Sicily and Magna Graecia. London, 1923

Buren, E. D. von
Greek Fictile Revetments in the Archaic period. London, 1926

Demangel, R.
La frise ionique. Paris, 1933

Goodyear, W. H.
Greek Refinements. Newhaven, 1912

Hambidge, J.
The Parthenon and other Greek Temples. Their Dynamic Symmetry. Newhaven, 1924

Kähler, H.
Das griechische Metopenbild. Munich, 1949

Koch, H.
Der griechisch-dorische Tempel. Marburg, 1951

Penrose, F. C.
An Investigation of the Principles of Athenian Architecture, 2nd ed. London, 1888

Puchstein, O.
Das ionische Kapitell. Berlin, 1887

Raphael, M.
Der dorische Tempel. Augsburg, 1930

Riemann, H.
Zum griechischen Peripteraltempel. Düren, 1935

Schede, M.
Antike Traufleisten-Ornamente. Strasburg, 1909

Schefold, K.
Das aeolische Kapitell (Jahreshefte Osterr. Archaeol. Inst., XXXI, 1939)

Shoe, L. T.
Profiles of Greek Mouldings. Vol. 1. Cambridge (Mass.), 1936. Vol. 2. American Academy, Rome, 1952

Solon, L. V.
Polychromy, Architectural and Structural. New York, 1924

Theuer, M.
Der griechisch-dorische Peripteraltempel. Berlin, 1918

Volkert, K.
Das Akroter. Vol. 1, Archaïsche Zeit. Düren, 1932

Weikert, C.
Das lesbische Kymation. Leipzig, 1913

Wiegand, Th.
Vorgeschichte des korinthischen Kapitells. Wurtzburg, 1920

Monuments

Athens

Balanos, N., Les Monuments de l'Acropole. Athens, 1930
Bohn, R., Die Propyläen der Akropolis zu Athen. 1882
Bundgaard, A., Mnesikles. 1957
Paton, J. M. and Stevens, G. P., The Erechtheum. 1927
Picard, Ch., L'Acropole d'Athènes. Paris, 1930
Bassae
Cockerell, C. R., The temples of Apollon Epicourios at Bassae, 1860
Dinsmoor, W. B., The temple of Apollon at Bassae (Metropolitan Museum Studies IV, 1933)
Corinth
Corinth. Results of Excavations. II-XV, 1932 sq.
Delos
Exploration archéologigue de Délos. 1 sq. 1909 sq.
Gallet de Santerre, H., Délos primitive et archaïque. Paris, 1958
Vallois, R., L'Architecture hellénique et héllenistique à Délos. Paris, 1944
Delphi
De La Coste-Messelière, P., Au Musée de Delphes. 1936
Fouilles de Delphes, II. Topographie et Architecture, 1915 sq.
Didyma
Knackfuss, H., Didyma, I. Die Baubeschreibung, 3 vol., 1942
Rehm, A., Didyma II. Die Inschriften. 1958
Eleusis
Noack, F., Eleusis. 1927
Epidaurus
Gerkan, A. von, Das Theater von Epidauros. Stuttgart, 1963
Roux, G., L'Architecture de l'Argolide aux IV et III siècles av. J.-C. Paris, 1961
Miletus
Miletus, 1903 sq.

Olympia
Olympia. Die Ergebnisse der deutschen Ausgrabungen. 5 vol., 1890-1897
Olympische Forschungen, Vol. I-V, 1945 sq.
Paestum
Krauss, F., Paestum. Die griechischen Tempel, 3rd ed. 1943
Krauss, F., Die Tempel von Paestum, I. Der Tempel der Athena 1958
Zanotti-Bianco, P. and Zancani-Montuoro, M., Heraion alle Foce del Sele, 4 vol., 1948 sq.
Pergamon
Die Altertümer von Pergamon. Berlin, 1885 sq.
Deubner, O., Das Asklepieion von Pergamon, 1938
Kähler, H., Pergamon. 1949
Priene
Gerkan, A. von, Das Theater von Priene. 1921
Wiegand Th. and Schrader, H., Priene. 1904
Samos
Reuther, O., Der Hera Tempel von Samos. 1957
Sicily
Hulot-Fougères, C., Sélinonte. Paris, 1910
Koldeway, R. and Puchstein, O., Die griechischen Tempel in Unteritalien und Sizilien. 1899
Marconi, P., Agrigento arcaica. Palermo, 1931
Tegea
Dugas, C. and Clemmensen, E., Le sanctuaire d'Athéna Aléa à Tégée. Paris, 1924

Acknowledgements

The photographer and publishers express their sincere thanks to Professor Dakaris in charge of Antiquities at Ioannina (Epirus) for allowing photographs to be taken on the site of Mesopotamon and for providing plans of the Necromanteion. They also wish to thank the Greek National Tourist Office and the Turkish Tourist Bureau in Berne for their helpful collaboration. Special acknowledgement is due to Olympic Airways for facilities accorded on their routes Zurich – Athens, and Athens – Ioannina. Several text drawings have been taken from the following books: **Manuel d'architecture grecque,** Vol. 1, by Roland Martin, A. and J. Picard, Paris; **L'urbanisme dans la Grèce Antique,** by Roland Martin, A. and J. Picard, Paris; **Griechische Tempel und Heiligtümer,** by H. Berve, G. Gruben and M. Hirmer, Hirmer, Munich. Grateful acknowledgement is made for loans made by them.

Table of Contents

Plates